Well it Seemed Like a Good Idea

Hugh Pilsworth

2021

Self-published in 2021 by Hugh Pilsworth
Melbourne, Victoria

Typesetting by Nicole Mays

Printed in Australia by IngramSpark

Enquiries should be made to the author at blueflyer4905@yahoo.ie

ISBN: 978-0-646-84242-4

A catalogue record for this book is available from the National Library of Australia

Cover images

Front cover: *BlueFlyer*

Rear cover: Hugh Pilsworth (author) and *BlueFlyer*

BlueFlyer

Introduction

This is the story of why and how I sailed my boat on a world circumnavigation over several years.

It was neither a non-stop voyage nor a solo one, but rather a series of shorter journeys with friends or acquaintances on board as crew members, changing over at mutually agreed times and places, most of these changeovers having been arranged pretty much before setting off at all. The plan also included exploring the places we stopped at and liked, and when we had time to do so. I had a route thought out, but we did not always stick to it, the weather and circumstances always interfere with sailing plans! Sometimes we did not have enough time at stopovers and sometimes we had too much time. On those occasions I would fly home or elsewhere and the leaving crew would depart and, on my return, the new crew would arrive.

The journey was in memory of my late wife who had sailed with me all of our married life and had accompanied me from Dublin, Ireland to Melbourne, Australia, and other voyages as well. It includes the story of how we bought the boat and then equipped her with extras, some of which were successful and some of which weren't so good, a bit like the journey itself.

For me, some of the journey involved sadness, being alone without my life companion Val who unfortunately developed Motor Neuron Disease. This is a terrible condition which gradually destroys the nerve connection to muscles. Val developed the head version which meant not being able to talk, swallow or eat.

My daughter, Fiona, and my granddaughters, Kiera and Eila, being so far away also increased the loneliness. Although the telephone and internet helped there were still many lonely times, especially when revisiting places that my wife and I had previously visited.

This is not a story of hardship and suffering, of adventures or mishaps. In fact, I went out of the way to circumvent as many of these pitfalls as possible, using modern navigation equipment and a weather router to avoid as many problems as possible, quite successfully with one or two exceptions.

This voyage was more an exploration of countries and islands linked by sea trips, rather than a long sea trip interrupted by landfalls. It was a trip involving meeting new people on land and putting up with sometimes insane shoreside procedures. Many of the boats and crews we met along the way would keep reappearing unexpectedly. It was also a period of mourning over three years, and of self-discovery, much as our voyage to Australia had been on our emigration trip from Ireland.

I'm often asked what's next. I am selling the boat in an effort to prevent any more long overseas sailing, but if she doesn't sell then who knows what's in store. I cannot visualise life without some sort of boat. Certainly, I have a hankering to sail around Cape Horn and in the Mediterranean Sea too, but one must always bear in mind that when Man plans, the Gods laugh! So who knows, watch this space!

Hugh Pilsworth
June 2021

Contents

Chapter 1 - Preparations

When my wife, Val, and I decided to replace our 29ft Dehler cruiser/racer in 2004 we were thinking in terms of something around 38 to 40 feet of cruising boat. Dublin Bay was our backyard and from there we could explore north and south along the east coast of Ireland, as well as the west coast of England, Scotland and Wales without much trouble or preparation.

We had already decided to sail across the Atlantic Ocean to the Caribbean with the Atlantic Rally for Cruisers and then ship the boat to Melbourne to join our daughter there, having secured the required residency visas already. This was to be our one and only ocean crossing. We started the process by selling the Dehler and then going shopping for a suitable replacement.

May I say at this point what fun is to be had at boat shows when you're in the market for a new boat, with cash in hand! We had our budget and enjoyed checking out a lot of very different boats on display at various boat shows. We soon found that the budget would stretch to a few 50 footers, fitted out to our requirements.

Eventually we both settled on the Jeanneau Sun Odyssey 49 through the Irish agents. We loved the look of her, sleek and low, and down below was amazing, all that space, with two showers and heads (toilet/washroom), and a real full size chart table too! Unbelievably luxurious to us after a 29 foot boat. I found the fit and finish of the boat to be excellent and, as it turned out, the hull and rigging were very strong too. The main, forward cabin, even had the shower and head en-suite, how good was that! There was adequate water storage for long voyages, but the fuel tankage was a bit small, we ended up with a dozen Gerry-cans on board to supplement the range under engine.

We already had a list of extras we wanted so that we could easily sail 2 up. So the primary winches were changed to electric, gates were fitted on both sides in the life lines and we specified teak laid decking as well. This always looks so good on bigger boats. I did have a look at a sister boat without the teak and thought that it looked incomplete. I also specified a 130% genoa, and a second VHF radio in the cockpit. As well as all that, I had a second chart plotter installed in the cockpit table, visible from both helms. I also had all the fittings needed for a spinnaker installed, and had a gennaker made.

We first saw *BlueFlyer* in the water in Les Sables-d'Olonne in France. After her commissioning was complete, we, with a crew of friends, sailed her back to Dublin. We encountered one or two problems along the way but all was fixed by the dealer.

When we got *BlueFlyer* back to our yacht club in Dublin we had two seasons to get her ready and for us to learn the boat, as we were planning to depart in July 2007 to arrive in the Canary Islands around early November. These two summers were spent cruising the Welsh coast and around Northern Ireland.

Val named the boat *BlueFlyer*, which has nothing to do with speed or colour but is the name given to a female Red Kangaroo in Australia.

First item to go on board was a 7kVA generator in the sail locker, not the ideal spot but it fitted in there with its own fuel tank. Next to go in was a desalination unit in the starboard lazarette, the stern locker. To do this I first removed all the wood panelling and installed a shelf and a horizontal floor, and then mounted the desalinator on the shelf. At all times I had to preserve the access to the steering mechanism in the same area.

I acquired two second-hand high footed Yankee jibs and had them altered to suit, along with two whisker (lightweight) poles to hold the jibs out in lighter downwind sailing.

The really major alteration from standard was done for me. This was to "CopperCoat" the underwater part of the hull. After 12 years this is still working, although it's thin to rubbed away in spots. I did this so as to prevent having to lift out in the Pacific Ocean to clean and re-apply antifouling paint. Oh yes, we were now going to sail all the way as I had found out the shipping costs from Miami to Melbourne, and the ARC organisers were now doing a Round the World trip.

Those were the major modifications we made before setting off.

~~~~~~~~
~~~~~~~~

After a reasonable trip of just over 12 months, we had the boat in Australia in 2009. I had the misfortune to damage my back mid Pacific by falling down the companionway steps. When we reached Tahiti, I could only walk a couple of steps, but I could cycle! I had a scan of my spine done which showed crushing of two vertebrae, so we left the boat with the agent in Tahiti and flew to Melbourne for a very successful operation, and, following recuperation, we rejoined the boat with new crew and two crutches for me and then sailed on, rejoining the rally in Fiji.

It took only 12 months in total to get to Cairns from Dublin, and then another 12 months to get to Sandringham, near Melbourne. Leaving Dublin we cruised down to the Canary Islands, spending time in England, France, Portugal and Spain before heading to St Lucia in the Caribbean area in time for Christmas. On the way into the Caribbean we had the misfortune to meet a hurricane, but that was survived with no problem. After this it was through the Panama Canal, Galapagos, French Polynesia and through Fiji and Vanuatu to Cairns in Australia.

~~~~~~~~~

In 2015 Val passed away from the Motor Neuron Disease and I then sold my house south of Melbourne and rented another with my daughter and her family, before deciding to sail off around the world as an escape from the loss I was feeling. Not having a house with all its associated problems was a real bonus and Fiona was happy to look after any mail, etc that might come.

So more preparations were needed/wished for:

I had the boom and mainsail replaced with a furling one, a new genoa was made, I bought a new movable Australian made desalination plant and had a diving compressor installed, along with a rack holding three scuba bottles. A new 5kVA generator was installed, in the saloon this time, much more accessible for maintenance. This was a much more compact diesel unit, with a new fuel tank constructed for it in the sail locker. Although this meant the loss of some storage space in the saloon and some noise in the saloon when it was running, these drawbacks were all acceptable to me.

On the safety side I bought a new life raft as the old one proved to be damaged beyond repair due to water getting inside the cover and rusting out the internals. An Emergency Position Indicator Radio Beacon (EPIRB) and four Personal Locator Beacons (PLB) as well as a tub full of new flares completed the safety fit out. The satellite phone and long range radio were still on board. I also bought an Iridium Go satellite unit so as to receive emails at sea.
~~~~~~~~~

For training three of us, Garry, Dawn and I attended a Safety at Sea course, which involved a morning studying in a classroom, followed by a session letting off flares and then an afternoon in the pool with life rafts, learning how to get into them fully clothed and how to right them, none of this is easy!

I also borrowed "Wendy" from the Sandringham Yacht Club for an afternoon's on water training for as many of the crew as could make it . "Wendy" is a life size dummy weighing about 85 kilos when wet. She floats head up and is a realistic man overboard rescue training aid. Several lessons were learnt from this session, including how difficult it can be to get the boat alongside the person in the water. We also decided that hooking a spare halyard onto the life jackets harness and using the electric winch was the best way to get someone out of the water.

As well as all that I serviced the winches and fitted a second hand "Walder" boom brake in place of the preventers that I had used previously. This is a resistive drum with rope wrapped onto it to slow down any violent, and potentially damaging, swings of the boom that may occur accidentally and thus prevent damage to the rigging.

The propeller and propeller shaft were treated with "PropSpeed" anti-foul and all new anodes fitted.

As well as these boat preparations I registered *BlueFlyer* as an Australian vessel. I spent some time organising and buying the relevant paper charts and updating all my electronic ones. So now the boat was ready, all I needed was crew.

I decided that the easiest way to arrange crew was to divide the voyage into legs. These were, approximately, the ocean crossings.

First though I had to get to Darwin, northern Australia, meeting up with the WARC again in Mackay during August. This link up would mean that I would complete the initial circumnavigation on arrival in the Caribbean.

I approached several friends in my yacht club with approximate dates and places, and a request to tell me if a) any of them were interested and b) when they might be available.

I also asked a Japanese guy who had crewed across the Pacific with me before. He was very happy to re-join the boat and we arranged to meet up in Mackay. I was surprised to get so many positive results, and filled all the crewing spots on board as far as Cape Town, South Africa. This really was about as far ahead as was practical to arrange.

After all that it was a matter of filling up with fuel and food and heading off.

Chapter 2 -
East Coast to Mackay

Melbourne to Sydney
6 June - 21 June 2016
Eric, Sharyn and Meg on board

Saturday 6 June 2016 had been decided on as the start date, subject as always, to the weather. As is well known in sailing circles, if you don't have a departure date set in advance you never leave the dockside.

After a noisy lunch in Sandringham Yacht Club, my family and a large bunch of friends strolled down to the boat which was still alongside the fuel dock, having topped up the diesel that morning.

It was a cool and misty day, not ideal, but these conditions were not going to delay our departure. It was winter after all and we reckoned on the conditions improving as we turned north. We weren't going far that day, just to the Queenscliff Cruising Yacht Club (QCYC) for the night. We let go the lines at 2.30 pm and, accompanied by several boats, and the infamous Sandringham trumpeter, we set off on the very first leg of this circumnavigation. We were soon on our own for the five hours of motoring. There were no problems on the way and we spent the night alongside at QCYC.

The next day the forecast was poor with easterlies predicted, and the fire in the yacht club was very attractive, so we remained tied up all day and set off at 7.50 am the following morning, motoring out of the skinny channel into Port Phillip and down to The Rip. This is the entrance to Port Phillip and can be very rough and not safe. However we went through without any problems and into the infamous Bass Strait. We turned left, heading SE towards Wilsons Promontory, the southernmost tip of mainland Australia.

We unfurled full sails, but the engine remained on as there was not much breeze. Weather was clear with good visibility, but chilly, something we would get used to! Lots of craypots around and pods of dolphins playing on the bow. The day passed peacefully leading into the first of many night shifts over the next few years. We rounded "The Prom" in the dark, staying inside the islands. The sky was clear and now it was definitely freezing cold on watch.

All the following day the seas in "The Paddock" between Wilsons Promontory and Gabo Island got rougher but no real increase in wind strength, but there was enough to turn off the engine and sail. It was quiet without the engine running. Mid-afternoon we passed through the oil platforms and sailed on to Gabo Island which was passed around midnight so we didn't see all that much of the SE corner of Australia. Our course then changed to northerly, aiming to reach Eden in daylight, which we did at 9.30 pm.

Eden was missing several navigation marks, and the long wood chip quay consisted of a crane sitting on its concrete platform in the middle of the bay. All the rest of the conveyor belt and support quay had been destroyed the previous week by a big SE storm, whilst we were tucked up in QCYC. The swell in the harbour was still running around four metres and even around the corner when we tied up to the commercial fisherman's wharf it was still rough, as was the wharf.

We tied up alongside as instructed by the harbour master and hopped ashore for a coffee, etc. I think this was the worst coffee I've ever tasted! Not recommended.

That evening a fishing boat came alongside and insisted we move out of his berth. No amount of discussion, or pointing out that we had been instructed to moor there would persuade him. In the end we moved a couple of boat lengths out of his way. Not a word of thanks was heard. As soon as that was done the barge board snapped with a very loud bang, so now all the fenders had to be reset to protect us from the wooden piles of the quay. Not a good night with checking the mooring lines and the fenders. There was some very minor damage to the boat that night.

Next day we bought a new barge board and two large, round orange fenders from the local chandlery shop and all was good.

Despite our intention to depart Eden the following day, we didn't as the forecast was for strong winds. These never eventuated so we had the pleasure of an evening meal in the off season. The only eatery we found open was the fish and chip take away shop, so that's what we had sitting in a local park huddled up in our warm jackets. As it happened the wind did not strengthen, but neither did it get any warmer. The talk was now of how much warmer Sydney would be!

Next morning, we left Eden at dawn, around 6.30 am, and out into flat seas and flat winds! This was in contrast to our arrival, but still very cold at about 3 degrees only. To be on the safe side I transferred 45 litres of fuel into the engine tank as we were obviously going to motor all day in these conditions, with the plan to get as far as Batemans Bay for the night.

It was uplifting and distracting to have the company of lots of whales who were also going north with us, obviously looking for the warmer waters as well.

We just made the tide over the bar at the entrance to Batemans Bay and onto the marina in the late afternoon. As we approached to tie up the wind gusted up to 20 knots plus, but we managed to land the boat without any further damage. I noticed quite a few developments and improvements in the harbour area compared to my previous visit several years prior.

That night we had a lovely meal, with wine, etc, in the marina restaurant and then retired to bed. One real plus to marinas is the shore power. This means I can run the air con/heater as needed on board, otherwise it's on with the generator. We did appreciate the gentle background heating all night.

Next morning was a late start due to tidal constraints. We waited outside the marina for about 30 minutes and then dredged our way out to the open sea again over numerous sand banks. The course was northerly again, heading up to Jervis Bay and the first of many nights at anchor.

This turned out to be a lovely sunny winters day with calm seas and more whales for company. However the downside of these conditions was having to listen to the engine all day. We did put the sails up to aid the engine, but there was not enough wind to turn off the engine. As the engine pushes the boat along the speed created a breeze over the boat. This is known as apparent wind and we used this, plus the real breeze of up to 5 knots, to help the engine and so reduce fuel usage.

Late afternoon we turned into Jervis Bay through the imposing heads and an hour later we anchored off the Hole in the Wall. Due to, I suppose, political shenanigans when Australia was united, this part of Jervis Bay is in the Australian Capital Territory (ACT). That evening, in the really calm water, the activity on board was dinner, drinks and sleep, a well deserved relaxing night.

Next morning was a lovely sunny day again, but still cold. However by 9.00 am we were off the anchor and heading out to sea with another yacht for company. Outside the bay was a bit lumpy and rolly, and it was motor-sailing again all day to Wollongong. No whales today until mid-afternoon for some reason. It took us just over eight hours to reach Wollongong and tie up to a visitor's buoy. All was well on board but at this stage we were all asking when the temperature would rise as it was still cold.

That evening we went ashore and met up with some friends of Meg's, and eventually found a suitable restaurant for dinner and beer. On returning to the dinghy the outboard engine refused to start, it really does need fuel! Eric rowed out to *BlueFlyer* and refuelled. Fortunately he then came back and ferried us back on board. Very nice of him!

By 9.00 am the next morning we were en route to Cronulla Marina. It was calm and clear again so more motor-sailing to the marina with lots of whales for company. At one stage we had to slow up to avoid a family of them! This was a short five hour trip with no problems. This marina is fairly new and spotlessly clean, with the very helpful staff on hand as we pulled in. The office is a floating house boat at the entrance. I arranged to stay here again on the way back. We went ashore and had a great meal at the local RSL restaurant followed by a walk around the headland and along the beach before returning to the boat. We stayed at this pleasant spot for a couple of days before the time was right to go to Sydney.

Soon enough we left and motored around to Sydney Harbour with Eric doing the steering in through the famous Heads and then on to tie up to the Cruising Yacht Club of Australia (CYCA) marina for crew change over and a rest. On the way in to the marina we paused at the neighbouring fuel dock and put 280 litres of very expensive diesel into the two tanks we had been using, not too bad considering the amount both the engine and generator had been used so far.

Next day Peter, Cheryl and Bernie arrived to take over as crew for the next leg as far as Mackay.

We spent a week in Sydney, doing touristy things. First was taking the boat past the Opera House, under the bridge and into Darling Harbour with both sets of crew on board. As always everyone looked at the mast top whilst going under the bridge. It never matters what the charts say the bridge height is, all on board still keep a watch. You never know if the bridge has sunk into the ground when no one was looking!

~~~~~~~~~
~~~~~~~~~

Sydney Opera House - 18 June 2016

Sydney to Mackay
21 June - 20 July 2016
Peter, Cheryl and Bernie on board

We said goodbye to Eric, Sharyn and Meg here. Meg has a house not far from Cronulla and was living in Sydney having left her job in Melbourne.

The temperatures had still not got anyway warm so we were all hoping that Coffs Harbour might be warmer and definitely by the time we got to Mackay even warmer still, surely? Cheryl also left before we set off, to re-join us in a couple of weeks' time; work is such a terrible occupation!

It was now 21 June and time to leave, having delayed a day or two to allow a Southerly Buster low pressure cell to go through.

9.30 am and we were motoring out through the Sydney Heads again, heading to the first stop at Newport Marina for the night. There was no rush as our only deadline was late August in Mackay to join up with the World ARC again after a nine year gap.

We actually managed to sail on leaving Sydney until we had to motor into Newport Marina. We dined in the Newport Hotel al fresco beside the fire pit that had been lit for the cold evening. Have I mentioned the temperature before?

Early the following morning we departed for Newcastle. We left the Pittwater area around 8.00 am and headed north again under sail only, no engine! What a pleasure it was to not have the engine running. Whales around still and after an uneventful trip we entered Newcastle mid-afternoon after a most pleasant day of sailing. We encountered our first commercial vessels too, a ship going in ahead of us and a dredger outbound.

Again the following day, having motored out, we had the sails doing all the work to get us as far as Port Stephens and the next stop. Our speed on these sailing legs was generally between 6.5 and 8 knots so, although we weren't rushing, nor were we dawdling along, always trying to reach the next stop in daylight, more pleasant to reach a destination with the sun still shining. It was beautiful sailing on a broad reach with more whales for company.

However the battery voltage was dropping alarmingly quickly, by mid-morning we were down to only 10 volts and so the generator was started to charge them up again. This was not meant to happen and whatever the problem was needed to be checked out urgently. We motored all the way in to the end of the bay and secured alongside a small marina there.

The next couple of very windy days were spent in Port Stephens and proved very expensive and cold too. A new battery charger and five new house batteries later and the marina electrician reckoned our problems were over, a mere $4,500 charge! Apparently the old American charger/inverter was only working on two of the three banks of batteries, and not fully charging any of them.

We departed the Anchorage Marina Sunday morning and motored out into the ocean, taking about an hour to reach the open seas again. Then it was motor-sailing again north to Tuncurry and the fisherman's wharf at the Co Op. It was raining as we left Port Stephens, the first time since before Gabo Island. We had to dodge several whales along the way, and after an uneventful day we motored in and tied up alongside the wharf. That evening we had dinner in the bowls club, a very pleasant meal, followed by an easy night back on board.

Next day was cold again with little wind, so we motor-sailed on to Camden Haven where we grabbed a spot on the jetty for the night. Before we all went ashore and had dinner at the United Serviceman's

Club, Eric and I swapped over the two gas bottles on board at the nearby service station. One was empty and the other had wrong connections on it. We had to be a little bit sneaky doing this as we weren't sure that the station would want a BBQ connection bottle. We noticed a neighbouring Jeanneau was from Williamstown in Melbourne but no one was present on board.

By 7.00 am the next morning we were back out with the genoa and engine pulling us along in quite strong winds, up to 40 knots at times. This kept up all day and we averaged 8.3 knots with a max of 12.3 according to the log. Our time of arrival at Trial Bay was just after 1.30 pm, much earlier than planned! It was both sunny and warmer here, maybe because we were well sheltered from the wind. A couple of other boats shared the anchorage with us but no one ventured from any of them. A peaceful night's sleep, after a very nice dinner on board.

Next day we sailed north to Coffs Harbour in lovely conditions, very different to the previous day. As the marina had been comprehensively trashed in the recent storm that had also damaged Eden, there were no berths on the marina. There wasn't all that much marina either. We grabbed one of the two mooring balls available in the inner harbour, near the old wharf running out into the harbour. This used to be a commercial loading wharf for all the hinterland produce in days long gone by but is now a walking pier for locals and visitors. We met Elise, the marina manager, in the local yacht club. She is the Ocean Cruising Club representative for the area and was very helpful too.

Without the marina we didn't feel like staying too long and so departed the following morning, next stop at the Clarence River town of Yamba, on the opposite side to Illuca. Nice sailing again, and we arrived at the entrance early afternoon. Yamba is upriver from the entrance so you have to motor upstream, keeping to the not very clearly marked channel. If you go the wrong way you end up in Illuca on the opposite bank instead of Yamba, not a great hardship. We went the right way, having been there before, and on the way into the marina I topped up the diesel again, 134 litres. We had dinner in a local restaurant, had another good night and then departed late, 10.45 am, the next morning having waited for the tide to rise enough to get out of the river. We still needed a short tow off a mudbank on the way out! Next stop was the Ballina public wharf. More motor-sailing as the wind was quite slack all the way.

It was now 1 July and we were well ahead of schedule, not that we actually had anything definite planned, other than the Mackay arrival date of mid-August. Although the notice on the public floating platform in Ballina said only two hours permitted, we all reckoned that nobody would enforce this so we went ashore to look around and have a very tasty dinner.

Next morning we departed Ballina, heading to Runaway Bay marina, a day's travel as normal. It was still cold, but we all said it'll be warmer in Brisbane soon enough. There was little wind again so we were motor-sailing in company with more whales at sea and some hot air balloons on shore. We arrived mid-afternoon and headed into the marina. This was obviously a motorboat area as we were one of only two yachts on the marina and we felt quite out of place, but were still made very welcome by the staff.

Next morning we entered the Broadwater, as this area is called. I don't know any other word to describe this waterway other than bedlam. There were boats everywhere travelling at all speeds. There were tinnies parked and drifting with people fishing and then there were also large power boats going as fast as possible in every direction. How we survived I don't know, but we were untouched. To top it off, I managed to put us aground briefly too. It was so good to be on the marina and tied up for the night.

Taking our lives in our hands we set off north the next morning through the Broadwater towards Brisbane. It was sunny and calm, and being inland waters, flat and peaceful. Then we went aground again on the falling tide in one of the many channels in amongst all the sandbanks. We waited some hours till the tide lifted us up again, but we couldn't find a way out, we kept finding sandbars everywhere we turned, so I called the VMR (Volunteer Marine Rescue) on the radio. To put the tin lid on this situation the poor old engine began to overheat due to being run hard to try to force a way out. A rescue boat appeared not long afterwards and even our combined efforts could not release us from the trap. We arranged that they would return on the next even higher tide the following evening.

We spent a day and night at approximately 40 degrees, not too comfortable but we survived. Sleeping can be a problem at this angle.

The next evening two rescue boats arrived to help. They spent about an hour surveying a route out and, on their return, we started the engine and followed them to an anchorage at Tiger Mullet Cove where we spent a peaceful night on anchor, and very enjoyable it was with the boat floating at the normal angle! We had found it strange to see towels hanging out from rails in the galley.

~~~~~~~~~~
~~~~~~~~~~

Stuck on a sandbank at approximately 40 degrees - 4 July 2016

On 5 July we upped anchor and travelled south and then out through the bar at Southport Tower. Peter was on the helm for this rough exit, good experience for him! Then a left turn and heading north again to Scarborough, just north of Brisbane. We were accompanied by dolphins and cold weather again, would it ever warm up, surely by Brisbane?

Nine hours of motor-sailing again got us to the east side of Moreton Island in the late evening darkness. I tried to go through the banks to the south of this big island, but ended up going north about to Moreton Bay and the shipping channel.

At this stage it was pitch black, overcast and very cold. As well as that there was an outgoing tide with a nasty chop that kept wetting us. At least the outgoing ships were contacting us on the radio and arranging which side we would pass each other. It was strange to see ships lights coming straight for us, knowing that the channel would take another twist or two before we met, scary if you've not been there before.

4.30 pm and we were tied up to the Scarborough marina having successfully negotiated the narrow channel through the sand into Scarborough Marina. We were really pleased to be there, and Cheryl rejoined us as well for a couple of weeks.

Whilst we were at the marina, I refuelled both tanks and generally checked over the boat. The new batteries were holding their charge much better that the old ones, and all seemed well on board.

After an enjoyable couple of days looking around and meeting friends from Sandringham, we left early Friday morning going north to Mooloolaba. It took four hours to clear the channel out of Moreton Bay and then another four hours of motoring before entering the marina at Mooloolaba. Bernie's brother and sister-in-law joined us for dinner in the local yacht club that night, followed by another peaceful night on board.

This was a brief overnight visit and next day we motored again to Wide Bay with its notorious bar. The Coast Guard gave us waypoints to cross which we did without any problem. Another yacht followed us through about 300 metres behind, obviously believing that we would run aground before he did! We motored on and round a sand spit into Pelican Bay to anchor for the night. Val and I had anchored here previously and so I knew this anchorage to be a good one and sheltered. We all sat in the cockpit watching four wheel drives ashore whilst sipping our evening drinks.

Next morning I put Peter on the helm to get us through the straights up to Urangan, good experience again for him and Cheryl for their trip north in their own boat. Cheryl was jumping around the boat with binoculars to her eyes, examining all the local wildlife, whilst Bernie was busy down in the galley producing a delicious lunch for us all. There were no problems during this channel passage other than being ahead of the tide, and so mid-afternoon we tied alongside the marina in Urangan, having had a great days motoring through the narrow and twisty channel.

Monday morning we were away, heading to Bundaberg, having topped off the water. We motored all the way as there was little wind and by 3.00 pm were in Bundaberg marina having been in company with dolphins and a turtle, as well as a rolly sea, but no problems encountered.

Dinner that night was in the marina restaurant and was good.

Next day we rented a car and did a little exploring in the area. Nothing too strenuous, but we did include the Bundaberg rum distillery and a tasting session. Nothing will persuade me that rum should be ingested, but I suspect it's probably good for getting rid of mosquitoes!

We had a late departure in the morning, nothing to do with the rum, and headed north for an overnight voyage to Rosslyn Bay Marina. We motored out of the channel, turned left and put up the sails in the light southerly breeze. This breeze was the reason we stayed the extra day. It was so pleasant to be travelling without the engine all day. This was the longest sail to date! We anchored in Bustard Bay for an hour or so and had dinner in peaceful conditions. We had another yacht, *Blue Bell* with us all day which was a pleasant change from our rather solitary journey so far.

After dinner the breeze was dying so we started up the engine with the headsail and ran like this all night to reach Hummocky Island just before the bright red dawn, having passed Cape Capricorn during the night, so we were now in the Tropics at last! Still waiting for conditions to warm up though! By 9.45 pm we were secured to the marina. It had been a long leg for all of us.

I had planned to leave the next day, but as it was blowing 30+ knots in the marina and dropping rain incessantly, 160 mm in Yeppoon during that week we found out later, we rented a car and went off exploring all day. We also spent a day in Rockhampton, travelling by bus, and missing the return one we wanted. No problem though, just an extra hour wait.

The third day was the highlight of our stay. Laundry all day in the marina! Little things become important when there's nothing else happening.

Eventually we got away on the Monday 18 July, next destination Mackay. We left at 6.30 am when it got light, with motor and sails working. At mid-morning we saw a seam unstitching itself in the Genoa so furled it away for repairs later.

The sea was rolly and cold all day, but sunny and bright weather. At 4.00 pm we anchored in Supply Bay for the night. Despite the roll we all slept well and the anchor kept us securely fastened. Peter took the opportunity to pull down the genoa and do a stitching job to hold the seam and prevent any further damage. Next morning we motored away and got as far as South Percy Island where we again anchored for another rolly night.

Wednesday saw us motor-sailing north, passing through the ships at anchor off Hay Point, all waiting to load up with coal for China. About 20 plus ships there.

Late that afternoon we motored into Mackay Marina at last. Now we would have a break, and change of crew as well.

We took off both the genoa and the gennaker sails and had them repaired professionally in Airlie Beach, there being no facilities in Mackay itself.

Bernie departed from the boat at this point and Shinichi joined us with the plan that he would stay for the rest of the trip. Alas that was not to be!

Over the next days several more WARC boats came in and the fleet gradually gathered, some leaving the rally here to explore the South

Pacific area, including New Zealand and Australia, and some re-joining from previous years. Peter and I took a break from the boat and flew back to Melbourne for a few days.

One drawback to Mackay is that the marina is several kilometres from the town itself, so car rental or bus journeys are needed to see anything, let alone to go provisioning. The marina has a couple of cars that are rented out cheaply, but for a couple of hours only, needless to say they are heavily booked in advance. A further slight problem is the tidal range. If you're provisioning it's necessary to know the state of the tide as the walkway down to the boats gets very steep twice a day! Runaway trolleys are not unknown here.

Dinner - 12 July 2016

Chapter 3 - Mackay to Darwin

Mackay to Abell Point, Airlie Beach
1 - 25 August 2016
Peter, Cheryl and Shin on board

On my return to *BlueFlyer* I met up with Shin again after a long gap. He had sailed from the Caribbean to Tahiti with me on my first Pacific crossing. He arrived on board before me, having travelled on a very tortuous route via several stops from Japan, taking almost a week!

I started on all the maintenance work, i.e., engine and generator servicing, cleaning around the bilges, my laundry, and all the other never ending necessities on a boat. Shin was also cleaning and polishing everything in sight. During the engine service one of the four bolts retaining the engine's sea water pump cover sheared off whilst I was checking the impeller. Now I knew there were spares ones on board somewhere. They should be in one of the boxes full of nuts, bolts, shackles, etc but there was no way I could find them, despite searching everywhere I thought they could be, so I went into Mackay where I was lucky to get six stainless steel ones, so I replaced all the original bronze ones and kept a couple of spares just in case. I wonder where they are now?

The last day of July I attended what was to be the first of many World ARC briefings. This one was telling us, all the skippers that is, what to expect on the next leg to Darwin. A member of the local yacht club had come too, and chatted to us all, having done this journey to Darwin and back several times. He explained the various routes and potential hazards on the way north. It turned out that this leg was not going to be as bad as we had all imagined. The charts are all good, but do make the route look complicated and everywhere has long since been surveyed accurately. The navigation marks were all in place and working as these are commercial shipping routes too. To add to our joy the weather forecast was also good for the next few days.

Monday, 1 August saw *BlueFlyer* depart from Mackay, heading to Shaw Island for the first night on anchor. This was still familiar territory to me as I had anchored here on the NW corner of the island previously. Initially we set off with the mainsail up and engine running to help, but by early afternoon we stopped pretending that the sail was doing anything other than flapping around. This was not what the forecast had promised. Shin started the fishing on this leg and he caught a very nice Spanish Mackerel. This he converted into Sushi and Sashimi for us, very tasty! He and Peter started a fishing competition between them.

After a restful night we left the anchorage and headed to Abell Point Marina, Airlie Beach in the Whitsundays group with both the engine and sails again. It wasn't till the afternoon that we finally got to stop the engine and sailed on till we reached the marina at Abell Point. There I tied up just in front of *Brizo*, a Discovery 55, being sailed by a lovely English couple, also with the rally.

That evening we met up with Eric again for dinner ashore. He had driven his truck and trailer some 150 kilometres just to see us! I had also been in touch with other Melbourne friends sailing in the neighbourhood and we met up the next day for lunch along with some of their relatives. A good time for all concerned. Whilst we were on the marina, I got a fender returned that I had lent to another boat in Mackay. After dinner Eric spent some hours asleep in his cab and then drove back the 150 kilometres!

In the end we spent four days in this beautiful area, sailing around each day and returning in the evenings. We loved the islands and the golden/ white sandy beaches that seemed to be everywhere. The beautiful weather helped too.

However, all good things come to an end, and so did this visit.

Abell Point to Bowen

We left on 5 August heading north again to our next stop at Bowling Green Bay. We got to sail most of the way again in a moderate breeze but a choppy sea. None of us envied the boat we passed heading south into the SE wind. Cheryl started singing at one stage as we were leaving the Whitsunday Islands behind, that was a first for all of us.

Early afternoon saw us approaching Bowen, with its small marina. On rounding the tall headland that protects the bay from easterly winds we got hit by a sudden blast of wind that broke the retaining clips for the Bimini. We threw away the broken pieces and tied the straps directly onto the eyes on deck. As I steered in through the skinny channel the wind accelerated up to Force 7, say approximately 55-60 kph on the beam, so we had a slight case of touch parking, but no damage done. We stayed the night there, dining ashore in a local cafe. It's not much of a place really, small and there for fishing only.

Bowen to Townsville

Next morning I motored out into the channel and then we sailed on, passing Abbot Point with a couple of tugs waiting for business. Pleasant sailing with a good SE breeze pushing us nicely. Just as the breeze began dropping, we arrived and anchored in Upstart Bay. Once we were secured, we had drinks, followed by dinner and a good night's sleep. It's so good to have an anchor that can be trusted! Mind you, I always put out a lot more chain than is needed, as someone once said, the chain is not much use to anyone sitting in the anchor locker.

Next day was motor-sailing again in a light breeze to Bowling Green Bay. This is basically in the middle of nowhere, but a very nice anchorage all the same.

On the next morning, 8 August, we were away again, north to Townsville and another marina. It was great not having to rush our trip. It meant we could stop at night if there was a suitable place within range, and that everyone got to sleep properly each night. That makes a great difference to morale and general cheerfulness. It took us just on six hours to get to Townsville, with a mix of sailing and motoring in light winds and flat seas. The marina here is a tight one for a 49 foot boat but I managed to park anyway without hitting anything in the process. Also on this marina was *Shanti,* another round the world boat from Sandringham Yacht Club, being sailed solo by Jacquie Hope, a friend of Bernie's and mine.

The yacht clubhouse here is modern and so that was where we ate that evening, having spent a few hours wandering around the town. It's an interesting spot, worth a visit if you're in the neighbourhood. Lovely old buildings and excellent murals/graffiti.

Townsville to Haycock Island

Next day was all motoring, no real wind to help us along. I steered us inside Magnetic Island, having come in past it from the south. Next was Rattlesnake Island, followed by Oysters Island and then into the Hinchinbrook Channel for the night, with no other boats in sight or heard on the radio. We finally anchored off Haycock Island in the middle of the channel, a very sheltered spot, for a really quiet and peaceful night.

The following morning the hills around us were shrouded in clouds, but that did not hide the crocodile swimming along about 20 metres from our stern, no swimming by the crew for some reason! All we could see initially were two vee wakes in the water from the eyes. This did not appear to worry the three men standing in a tinny happily fishing away. We motored on to Brammo Bay, no wind, no fish caught and no whales, but we did dive after lunch. This was at Dunk Island, a well known resort island that had been thoroughly trashed by a cyclone a few years before. There was a newish jetty and a lot of ruined resort bungalows to visit. There were several groups of people camping in the area and it appeared that the public toilets were still working, but no reclamation work seemed to have been done. There was no money to do any work apparently as the previous owner is supposed to have taken the insurance payout and then sold up and disappeared.

Haycock Island to Cairns

We left the next morning at daybreak, 5.00 am and planned to get to Cairns that evening. This was yet another motoring day. We tried the sails for a while, but it was a waste of time. Along the way I drained out the forward fuel tank as it was still weeping diesel into the bilges and making the boat smelly too. That had the effect of putting about 60 litres of diesel into the main tank, through the bypass pipe arrangement I had installed before leaving Melbourne, enough to get us to Cairns without touching the reserve jerrycans.

By midday we were at Fitzroy Island at the end of the Grafton Passage. This pass is where we came through the reef previously. We entered the 5 mile long and very narrow channel heading to Marlin Marina, where we spent a total of five days, with Peter doing trojan work for a lot of the time. He cut out the front fuel tank, which had been constructed of wood and had not had a fuel proof membrane fitted, thus the weeping, then cleaned up the whole area before installing a new 100 litre plastic tank, all in the heat and high humidity of the tropics, not easy. Thanks to the local Ocean Cruising Club Port Officer for all the help he gave us on this project. We ended up having to stand the tank up vertically as it would not quite fit horizontally, so no fuel gauge, but we can see the diesel level through the plastic. Once all the pipe work had been modified and reconnected, I ran the generator and then filled the tank with new diesel. So good not to have a leaky tank and no smell.

The Ocean Cruising Club Port officer was marvellous. Once I found that the local Whitworths chandlery had a suitable tank in stock he piled us into his car and brought us around the various shops to get all the bits needed, and then back to the boat again. We had dinner with him and his wife later as a thank you from me for going so much out of his way.

There were several rally boats here at the same time so a get together was organised on the marina. Very sociable with some alcohol consumed.

Cairns was where *BlueFlyer* had first landed in Australia in 2008 and so from now on I was sailing in unknown waters. I was keeping my fingers crossed that the briefing in Mackay had been correct and that the route was a lot easier than it looked.

Cairns to Lizard Island

Now it's 16 August and we're off again. A late afternoon start under engine until we got out of the entrance channel. At night the green, starboard, and red, port, lights marking the channel all flash together, bar one port light which is out of phase. I wonder if the bulb had been replaced?

We put out the genoa and turned off the engine. Although it was raining, it wasn't cold, finally. Sea conditions were a bit ordinary in the solid southerly wind, about force 4-5 and the night was dark. My plan was to head into Cooktown for the night but conditions didn't allow for a safe entry so we carried on into the unknown, having changed onto a new course due to a wind shift to the SW for a while before it reverted back to the SE. Come daybreak and we put a couple of rolls in the genoa. We had been sailing along all night at around 6 knots and all was well on board. A couple of hours later the wind was gusting to 40 knots so we headed to Lizard Island for lunch at anchor.

There were eight or nine other boats anchored there as well, all waiting for the southerly winds to change to northerlies so that they could head south. We had a look at the luxury resort on the island, but it didn't look like anything special through the binoculars. After lunch the wind decided that we would remain here at anchor. We all had a reasonable night's sleep and after breakfast set off north again, under sail once more!

Lizard Island to Morris Inlet

As we passed Eagle Island Peter caught a bonito, and then lost it! Ah well that's fishing for you. Of course, it was a huge fish that got away! Lovely sailing with just the genoa all the way out and the sun shining brightly. Lunch time came and we put up the mainsail in conjunction with the polled-out headsail. On rounding Cape Melville in the late afternoon we put a reef in the main so as to be set up for the night. The Cape has an amazing boulder field on it, and there was a whale for company as well. We hadn't spotted any since before Cairns so that was a welcome sight.

There were several fishing trawlers in our neighbourhood so we had to keep a careful watch on them, you can never be certain what they're doing. By 9.00 am the next morning, after an uneventful night, we had anchored at Morris Islet. This is a small island of coral with a big but shallow lagoon. Peter rowed himself ashore and walked a full circumnavigation, enjoying all the guano that had been deposited everywhere. He now claims the record for a senior circumnavigation of the island by foot!

Morris Inlet to Darwin

After lunch we set off again under sail only. We had beautiful conditions and great visibility, easily able to see several ships passing both ways, with no problems missing them as there was plenty of channel width available. We passed around several reefs and then rounded Cape Grenville. Our heading became slightly west of north for a change due to the shape of the land having kept us east of north most of the way up the east coast. At this stage we were, of course, well into the sheltered waters between the Great Barrier Reef and the mainland and so had reasonable seas with us. The channel was well marked for all the commercial shipping and so caused us no navigational problems, other than remembering to vary the course as needed.

At 8.00 am on 20 August we dropped the anchor in Margaret Bay in company with a couple of catamarans. We spent a very peaceful day here in the flat waters and warm sunshine till we set off again in the evening after dinner on board. We passed various islands as we made our way north towards Cape York and the northernmost tip of Australia. We were, once again, motor-sailing. After a peaceful night's travel, we were approaching the Albany Channel. This channel is a gorgeous route to travel between the island and Australia, and a useful shortcut too. We dropped the sails as the breeze was not suitable to sail through and motored slowly through this amazingly beautiful channel. There are several places to anchor and one or two houses on shore too. By 9.30 pm the next day we were rounding Cape York, the most northerly tip of Australia. I found this a disappointing headland as it just slopes down to the sea with a car park and toilets visible on shore. The island off this tip is quite a sight though, with its lighthouse and reasonably steep slopes.

Now our heading finally changed to westerly at last. The east coast is a very long one when you're sailing and in no rush.

I set a course for Gove, about 350 miles away on the western side of the Gulf of Carpentaria. As we passed through the islands and sandbanks off Cape York and all the aboriginal settlements in the Torres Strait en route to Gove, we all remarked as to how beautiful the area was and how clear and blue the water was. This is all unspoilt territory belonging to the aboriginal communities. You need permission from both the owners and the government to stop here and go ashore. However if you do so you run into problems with bureaucracy and clearances, so we didn't stop. As we headed west the wind lightened, we had to sail further north than west so Gove was abandoned as a stopover. Next then we headed off for the Hole in the Wall passage about 250 miles further on in the Wessel Islands. As we were travelling along very happily, we started to get some electronic problems, the AIS packed up, that's the Automatic Identification System, and then the screen on the chart plotter would go blank now and again. Not knowing what else to do I rebooted the whole system, a technical term for switching off and then back on, and checked the settings on the plotter and it all settled down again, thank goodness.

Peter caught a fish again, so he was definitely in the lead for the fishing competition!

That evening the wind died considerably so it was back on with the engine and down with the sails. It stayed like that all night until we put the genoa back out in the morning. We kept on heading for the North Wessel Islands, about half way between Cape York and Darwin. Course still due west. On this leg several fish were caught and consumed, but there were more lures lost than fish caught!

We kept on motor-sailing in the flat seas, enjoying the moon and stars and the warm sunshine. Lovely conditions to be at sea.

Having had to abandon Gove as a stopover, we were now pushed north again by the conditions and ended up going north of the Wessels, so no Hole in the Wall passage on this trip. Such a shame as I'm told it's a spectacular gorge and a great shortcut to Darwin.

Thursday the 25th and we had *Odysseus* for company, about 5 miles off our starboard. That night we passed Cape Don, still with *Odysseus* and still motor-sailing. Our diesel supply was getting a bit low at this stage and I was anxious to do as much sailing from now on as possible.

Very early the next morning we sailed past Cape Hokam and we could all smell smoke from the land wafting our way. An alien smell to us now! To make up for this I baked some bread, but it rose too high in the oven and didn't cook properly. It was quite a job to get it out as it had jammed itself against the top of the oven! We also had our first overflight by Border Patrol, checking out who we were and where we were heading. We chose to travel through the inshore route to Darwin as we had daylight and the navigation did not seem too problematic.

Because of the 7 metre tidal range on this north coast, all the Darwin marinas have locks to get in and out. This preserves the water level inside the marinas, but also means that at about half tide the marinas shut up shop and no one can get in or out. Needless to say we were too late arriving and so ended up motoring around to Fanny Bay where we anchored for the night.

The following morning we motored up to the Tipperary Waters marina lock to get in. The lock looked to be a very tight fit for *BlueFlyer* but we made it OK, no damage sustained. After we tied up in the marina, I had a look out over the lock and it was an odd feeling to look out over the sea, about 6 metres below us at low water and see all the shallow areas appearing as the tide dropped. I'm not sure how we missed them!

The bow thruster control had been acting up so I got a local marine electrician to come over and test the system. He confirmed my diagnosis of a faulty switch at the helm and ordered a new one. We were very lucky that there was one available in Australia and it was promptly dispatched, arriving before the rally was due to leave. The electrician was very quickly on board with it and fitting was a minor job, so all was well again.

Peter and I left Shin in charge whilst we took a flight back to Melbourne to see our families and recharge our batteries.

Darwin
28 August - 5 September 2016
Peter, Cheryl and Shin on board

On our return to the boat, with Cheryl once more, we prepared for our first long overseas trip to Indonesia. We all went shopping for provisions, filled up the water tanks and then on the last night went out for dinner. Unfortunately this did not go at all well, with Shin arguing about navigation and saying that we were not ready to go. On returning to the boat this disagreement got worse and in the end I called in the police to check over the boat as Shin was now saying that there was a smell of drugs in his cabin, not what you want to hear when heading to Indonesia where drug smugglers are either shot or have long prison sentences. The police could not find anything and left with Shin and all his belongings at about 3.00 am in the morning! I arranged for Border Force to check us as well before departure.

Chapter 4 - Darwin to Lombok

6 - 18 September 2016
Peter and Cheryl on board

So now we were the three nautical travellers heading out to sea, but not in a pea green boat this time. I phoned Garry and Dawn in Melbourne to check that they would be happy to have only three on board for the Indian Ocean leg, fortunately they were.

Departure was about 9.30 am on 6 September. On board with me were Peter and Cheryl for the approximately six to seven day trip to the first foreign destination. Also on board was a surplus amount of food! As well as all we had laid in whilst in Darwin, there was also a goodly stash of tinned foods buried down in the bilges, and a lot of bottled water. I managed to reuse a lot of these bottles several times as they were emptied. Some we refilled with tank water and some were used to hold the waste oil from the engine and generator services.

After the Border Force customs arrived, with a sniffer dog, I explained the situation to them, and that our destination was Indonesia. They were happy to check over the boat and ensure that there were no drugs anywhere on board. After completing the very thorough examination we were cleared to sail. We were in time to go through the lock again with the other boats on the rally. We finally got to open water and headed off to the start line.

11.00 am was the official rally start time, with the sail training ship *Young Endeavour* in company. We managed to sail across the start, but a few hours later the engine was on and we were motor-sailing again, the forecast was for more of the same slack winds and flat seas so we were resigned to plenty of motor -sailing once more.

Our destination was in Lombok at the Marina del Ray in the south west corner of the island. We had been informed at the skippers briefing that, despite the name, there was no marina! The name had been chosen for a possible future development.

As we departed Darwin there was a Collins class submarine and a patrol vessel to our starboard entering the port which, with the *Young Endeavour*, Australia's tall ship training vessel, made a great navy escort.

We had some lovely sailing for a couple of hours, but then the wind dropped out and the engine came back on again. We watched a turtle diving for lunch on a jellyfish and that was about it as far as excitement went, but then we didn't want excitement or adventure along the way.

Every day after departure until we were almost at Lombok we were overflown by the Border Patrol in one of their security patrol planes and every day we answered the same questions; who we were, how many on board and our destination.

That night we had *Odysseus* in company again. This was the Beneteau 49 with an east European crew on board with whom we had shared several beers and nibbles on the marina in Darwin, a really friendly bunch of men.

Next morning we had the Border Force Patrol fly over us again, and a couple of sea snakes in company! Also we had a visit from some dolphins, playing around the bow as normal. We spoke to *Overseas Express* on the long-range (HF) radio, otherwise known as the SSB (Single Side Band). We had been having reception problems with this but having checked all I could behind the instrument panel I crawled down into the lazaret, or stern locker, and dismantled all the aerial and ground connections, cleaned them and then remade all the connections. This seemed to fix that problem. *Overseas Express* was a Norwegian boat being sailed by a lovely couple with excellent English, just as well as my Norwegian was non-existent.

Still motor-sailing along in a fickle breeze, the log showed a wind force between 1 and 0! That evening the breeze went up to about force 2, and we were hitting up to 6 knots of boat speed, the excitement was almost overwhelming.

By 10.00 pm that night we had shut off the engine finally and were under full sail, in company with dolphins again and phosphorescence, this looks great on a dark night, especially when flushing the toilets and as the water goes out the engine exhaust.

We managed to sail all that night with a gentle SW breeze until about 8.30 am in the morning of the third day out of Darwin when the breeze vanished again. As usual the Border Force Patrol flew over asking the same questions of various boats.

Unbelievably from now till our arrival In Lombok the engine never stopped! It got to be a background noise after a while but it's so annoying to have to keep using it. The conditions were really hot and muggy, quite unpleasant, so, as you can imagine, the saloon and cabins got rather warm and the heat from the engine was no help. Thank goodness we didn't have anything strenuous needing attention, I don't think it would have happened!

We carried on like this for the next day or two, discovering from Cheryl that she really does not like the thought of deep waters. On questioning her we found that deep means anything over about 2 metres! Just as well the depth sounder shows a maximum depth of only 104 metres, after that the signal is too weak to bounce off the sea floor.

The fifth day came with the Border Force Patrol again, and some excitement. On the SSB daily roll call came a call for anybody who could to stand by *Odysseus* as they had lost their engine to a problem that turned out to be terminal.

We rendezvoused with *Into the Blue* and stooged around until the situation was clear. We were many miles ahead of *Odysseus* and *Katerina*, a catamaran from Melbourne, was sailing back to give *Odysseus* a tow. The crew on *Katerina* were concerned that they might not have enough diesel to tow the whole way and asked anybody around to stand by with spare diesel. On meeting up with *Odysseus* Tony on *Katerina* arranged a fuel transfer from *Odysseus* as they had spare fuel on board. Tony then found out that the rigging supporting *Odysseus's* mast was also damaged so the boat could neither motor nor sail! Not a pleasant situation to be in out at sea. The two boats transferred the fuel and arranged the towing bridle, thus beginning a long journey to Lombok at slow speed. A situation like this demonstrates one advantage of being in a rally.

As it now appeared that the situation was under control both *Into the Blue* and *BlueFlyer* set off again, much to Cheryl's relief!

That afternoon as we were cruising along at about 6-7 knots we hit something. No idea what it was other than being large and brown, fortunately doing no damage. It missed the keel and hit the rudder. As there was no apparent damage we decided not to stop and examine the boat and so we kept going, being careful not to strain the rudder until I was happy that it was OK.

Lombok was in sight the next morning and we kept on going west with *Into the Blue* and *Barbara Jean* just ahead, and staying in radio touch with Tony and Guinilla on *Katerina* who were making steady, if not speedy, progress towards Lombok, sailing as well as motoring which reduced their fuel consumption considerably.

We crossed over the finish line at 9.00 pm on 13 September after a fairly boring trip for us and went on into the bay to anchor. We had been strongly advised not to try this in the dark as there were so many obstacles in the way. Even in daylight the route was confusing and very convoluted with fish farms, unmarked naturally, and shallows to avoid.

We stayed here for five days exploring the island and I have to say that this is a beautiful area with many historic sites to look at and lots of restaurants as well. However, my lasting impression is of litter everywhere you look. As well as our tourist time ashore we spent time doing all the usual checks on board as well as refuelling. This was done from 45 gallon drums on a local boat, with an electric pump thank goodness, that came alongside. About half way through filling us the last drum ran dry so we waited whilst the drums were refilled ashore, reflecting that at least that means fresh and clean diesel.

Peter and Cheryl left the boat here and had a night or two in a local hotel, very comfortable too. From there we said goodbye as they were flying home, it had been great having them on board for their first overseas sail, as well as Peter having done a lot of the east and north coasts.

In the meantime, Dawn and Garry had flown in from Melbourne to join the boat for the next leg all the way to Cape Town across the Indian Ocean. They too stayed in a hotel for a couple of nights, overlooking the anchorage. However, even though they were "upgraded" to a superior room over the water, they could still see through the floor and they could also see the toilet outlet about 10 metres further out in the water! The toilet worked once and then they realised why there was a bucket in their room.

The electricity was available whenever the owner was bothered to start up the generator as there was no mains power connection at all. Similarly, there was no refrigerator or freezer. Everything that needed to be cooled, such as the beer, was kept in a couple of big Eskys filled with ice. Food was tasty but very limited in range, lots of fish though. There was no such thing as Internet here, so we used to go around by dinghy to Peter and Cheryl's hotel for that, and a beer or two, about a 20 minute journey.

Eventually *Odysseus* and *Katerina* arrived to much praise, and *Katerina* was awarded the 'Spirit of the Rally' award for their effort.

We enjoyed our time here, bus tours and visits to the nearest town where we all became millionaires instantly on changing $200 into the local currency. Apparently, the government is having long debates about taking a zero off all the denominations, at least then you would not be walking around with great wads of paper in your pockets. I managed to leave my bank debit card in the ATM on the first morning there, but got it back before leaving thanks to the bank head office and a lift from one of the officials. I think it was the shock of having so much money at one go!

There is no OH&S here, so for example when we came across a road being repaired there was a guy sitting on a stool in the middle of the road. His job was a bit undetermined but maybe he was there to warn the traffic, who knows?

A market in Lombok - 14 September 2016

Chapter 5 - Lombok to Cape Town

18 September - 27 November 2016
Garry and Dawn on board

Lombok to Christmas Island

Sunday, 18 September was the date chosen for the rally to depart from Lombok, heading across the Indian Ocean to Cape Town, South Africa, staying well south of Madagascar and its troubled waters that stretch about 200 miles south of the island. This leg, with several stopovers at islands along the way, would be approximately 5,500 miles in length and just over two months in duration, quite some journey for Dawn and Garry's first ocean voyage, and the longest single leg I had done too. This long and potentially hazardous voyage into the unknown did not appear to phase either of them, despite the Indian Ocean's fearsome reputation.

As had become normal we motored out to the start line with all of the other rally participants. There was absolutely no wind and without any breeze it felt very warm indeed. As a result this was declared to be a motor start. Just to be different I decided to cross the line going astern, I had no reason to do so, I just felt like it. Despite warning boats around this manoeuvre caused a few strange looks in our direction. At least Dawn and Garry now had some idea of what to expect.

After the start we motored on so as to get clear through the Lombok Strait in daylight due to there always being big logs and other such obstacles present. As well as these solid obstacles there was garbage from fishing boats of all sizes and shapes. When the families ashore run out of storage space, they dump the refuse bags when they're full into the boats and then drop the bags of rubbish overboard to let the tidal flow carry them away! Out of sight means not my problem.

After lunch we put up the sails and had a lovely quiet cruise for a few hours, then the wind went for a holiday again. Sails away and the engine was back on until early the next morning. At that stage we had enough breeze to put out the headsail and turn off the motor again. During the day the wind gradually picked up and eventually we had full sails up and were moving along nicely at 6 -7 knots in a South Easterly of about 18 knots, ideal for *BlueFlyer* under sail.

The sea was calm and a deep blue again as we moved further offshore and into deep water. We saw some dolphins that evening and Dawn got hit by a flying fish whilst on watch! Quite a shock when that happens to you, and they stink too! This fright is on a par with the dolphins who sneak up in the middle of the night and breath heavily next to the boat. That can be very scary as you know there's no one else up in the cockpit.

The next few days passed fairly uneventfully. Major excitement came when a seagull perched on the genoa pole for a while, and then one of the arms on the boom brake twisted itself up as the retaining rope jammed. Garry went up on the cabin roof and unbolted the damaged arm. We then managed to straighten it out and refit it to the boom brake again. I decided I would see if it was possible to get new and stronger arms made up somewhere along our journey.

We also had a heavy rainstorm or two with the wind gusting up to 30 knots, but generally benign conditions with east to SE winds of force 3-4 and reasonably calm seas, trade winds and not the conditions we anticipated, thank goodness. We were making good speed towards our first stop at Christmas Island in these lovely trade wind conditions. We had one period of three days without touching the sails, that's how steady the Trade Winds can be! Christmas Island is an Australian overseas territory with its own system of government, and a refugee centre for boat people trying to get into Australia illegally.

On 22 September we sighted the island and sailed happily into Flying Fish Cove where we picked up a mooring in the bay. 600 miles in four days, so not too dusty. These moorings had been laid specifically for the rally using mooring balls that were big, about 1 metre diameter, orange plastic ones and, as we discovered later, they had a habit of banging off the hull, not conducive to good sleep, in the ever present swell, and leaving orange-coloured marks on the white hull. One of the bigger boats, an Oyster, actually ended up dragging the mooring along the seabed when the wind got up.

There is no harbour on this island, so all ships moor off the land so as to not suffer damage in the swell. Part of the harbour is reserved for commercial shipping only with really big mooring balls attached to heavy weights on the sea floor. The yachts had a mooring field separated from this commercial area.

Once on shore, via the dinghy, we cleared in. Garry was soon to learn about the rainfall here as the dinghy needed bailing out every time we wanted to use it! We were now back in Australia again, after the usual tedious formalities, we were free to explore this tropical, volcanic island.

I located the local engineering shop, actually the only one, not too difficult to find as it was at the end of the landing platform and is called Christmas Island Engineering! They had a look at the boom brake arms and agreed to make me new ones. These are still in use and have been a great improvement on the originals. There was a small misunderstanding regarding the hole dimension for the ropes to run through but that was soon cleared up.

Next day we all piled into a tour bus arranged by the rally to have a look around this small island. The main items of interest were the refugee centre and the red crabs. The centre was discretely tucked away and was not really visible from the road, unless you have a reason to visit there. Despite also being boat people none of us were invited to stay! Apparently, all the locals were pleased when the centre was set up as all their infrastructure was upgraded! Reliable power and phone and internet communication with Australia.

The red crabs number in the millions and live up on the hills in the rain forest. Due to the height of the island this is temperate forest, not tropical. Once a year they migrate down to the seashore to reproduce. This is done at the same spot every year and apparently the migration is like a moving carpet. As these crabs are protected there are stiff penalties for driving over them. There are other crabs there too, such as the Robber crabs, but in nothing like the same numbers.

We decided to spend a few nights ashore in a hotel for a break from the never ending swell and banging of the mooring ball. Whilst we were there it rained. Not like normal rain, but the heavy tropical variety. As a result, we spent a couple of nights ashore, longer than planned, but had a lovely time exploring the local shops and cafes. It's a tough life sailing.

On our return to the dinghy, we found it full to the top with rain water and the spare petrol container on a beach several hundred metres away. Garry spent about 30 minutes bailing out all the water and Dawn went off to rescue the petrol can. There were a few scrapes on the outboard but no real damage and so we got back to *BlueFlyer* safely.

After five very enjoyable days here we set off again, having waited for the conditions to settle down a bit. Apparently, there are three social layers here with the Muslim people living at sea level, followed by Indians half way up and the Chinese at the top in the town. All very organised.

Christmas Island to Cocos (Keeling) Islands

We were heading next to the Cocos (Keeling) Islands about three days away, another Australian overseas territory. Some of the fleet departed before us and had been forced to return when they were tossed around by the wind and waves off the island. When we departed it seemed a lot calmer, until we left the lee of the island. Then the rain returned and the sea became lumpy and confused, probably due to the effect of the high hill. We ploughed on through this knowing that the conditions would improve soon. We knew this as the weather router had told us.

As the conditions improved, we put the sails out with a reef in the main and were tramping along at between 6 and 8 knots in a good force 5 SE breeze, no engine! This carried on for a couple of days. On 29 September the generator refused to start, but we were nearly there anyway so I just used the engine for charging.

The following day we arrived at the Cocos (Keeling) Islands, stunningly beautiful atolls with golden sands and crystal-clear waters. Again these are Australian offshore islands, also self-governing.

There is only one area where visiting boats are allowed to anchor, and that is at Direction Island. Navigation in is by eyeball so as to miss the bommies and reefs that are everywhere. Once in though there's a big enough anchorage area, with crystal clear water and good holding for the anchor in sand. The water is shallow enough to be able to see the anchor on the seabed.

Travel between the islands is either by your own dinghy or by the ferry from the hotel on one of the other islands. The distances, though not great, were still too big for our little dinghy and outboard to cover. The ferry is primarily for the hotel guests and so the timing is not suitable for visiting yachts. You can catch it in the morning to get to Home Island, but there's no return trip! Home Island is the main settlement and has all the facilities there, such as a small shop and the fuel depot. This is not a major town, with a much smaller population than Christmas Island.

On Direction Island there is a memorial to a First World War sea battle that occurred just off the island when the Royal Navy caught up with the German cruiser, *Emden*. The German was destroying the telegraph cable node on the island. This was the cable connecting Australia to the United Kingdom and the rest of the world and so was of great strategic value.

Also on the island is a phone box, put there by Telstra, and housing an extremely slow and extraordinarily expensive satellite internet connection. Most people gave up trying to use it.

There is a flight from Perth to here, on a weekly basis, which then goes onto Christmas Island. However, if the weather is bad anywhere along the route, there is no flight. As a result, when one does arrive, with food etc, there is sometimes a lottery both here and on Christmas to see who gets to travel! The delays can be up to a couple of weeks duration.

The sea here was a pristine aqua marine blue and it was quite easy to see the colourful fish and small sharks that abound. You could see what was swimming in the water, such as the lemon sharks that kept coming to the transom every day. Dawn and Garry had a great time swimming and snorkelling in the lagoon, and doing a drift swim in a pass, hanging onto a rope whilst the local wildlife swam past.

I traced the generator fault to a poor oil pressure sensor connection and fixed it easily enough. To test it I ran the water maker for the first time and filled all the water tanks in a couple of hours. I also found the sea water pump was leaking all over the alternator, but not having any spare seals, all I could do was make a shield from alu-foil to protect it and then wash off the salt, not satisfactory but I had no seals on board and wasn't going to find them out here. Each time I checked the genset from now on it got cleaned and sprayed with WD40.

Cocos (Keeling) Islands to Mauritius

After five beautiful days on this wonderful atoll, we reluctantly set off again on 4 October for the 2,400 mile trip to Mauritius Island. This would be a 15 day trip across the open ocean.

We sailed happily for the next couple of days in the SE trade winds without disturbing the engine at all. Blissful conditions. I did have to run the generator for up to 4 hours a day to recharge the batteries, but this coincided with tea times and cooking times.

We were travelling in company with some of the other rally boats for a couple of days but eventually we all separated and went our own routes. We put on the engine for a couple of hours one evening when the wind dropped out, but that was a temporary aberration on this leg. On the morning of the 6th Garry put up the gennaker. This is a big lightweight and colourful sail with good power in light breezes. It was up for most of the day until the light wind went even lighter and so the motor-sailing started again but only for a few hours. This was followed by a couple of days of sailing with full sails in SE winds of force 4-5 giving us good boat speeds of around 7 knots most of the time.

After a couple of days of these conditions the sea got up and became lumpy, but we were still sailing along nicely.

During this period the gas bottle ran out so I had to change over to the spare. Thanks to Murphy's law a wave came over the cockpit behind me whilst the gas locker was open. I had water up to my chest and I had to catch the empty bottle as it was trying to float away. Fortunately, the water was warm at around 30 degrees, but Dawn had a great laugh as we were both soaked to the skin. Garry, who was below cooking breakfast, wondered where all the water pouring down the companionway was coming from! The bilge pump took care of it all rapidly, there are three of them on board, two electric automatic ones, and one manual one operated from the cockpit.

After that little mishap the conditions improved and we carried on sailing, mainly just with the big genoa out in the now ESE wind. We left the main rolled up so as to prevent the big foresail being blanketed and also if we accidentally gybed there would not be any damage to the rigging. Winds were averaging force 5-6 and so we were rolling along at a good clip, and I do mean rolling, it never stopped, about 20 degrees each way. Very wearing!

The conditions stayed benign for us until the 12th when it rained! We had got used to warm sunny days and clear starry nights, so this was a shock to us all.

I had to change over the water tanks as the front one we had been using since the Cocos was finally empty. There are two forward tanks and one aft. All of them are about 240 litre capacity so we now were ¼ tonne lighter in the bow. I changed to the aft tank, keeping the other forward one in reserve.

Despite having a fishing line out most days it appeared that the fish were safe from us as none were caught. Garry changed the lures several times to no avail. Finally, late one afternoon we caught a fish, a Spanish Mackerel. Lovely fish for eating. The fish was filleted on the back step and half of these fillets went into the fridge, and the other half became dinner that night. What a lovely change to have fresh food for dinner.

We were in long range radio contact with the rally every morning at 9 o'clock, giving our position and conditions report. The positions were then passed on to the WARC people in the United Kiingdom. One advantage of a rally is the security of knowing that someone knows where you are. As well as this roll call, we all carried satellite trackers on board that sent our positions every 6 hours via satellite to anyone who cared to look.

All was going well and we were really enjoying this trip, the weather and sea conditions had been mostly excellent and not at all what had been anticipated before leaving Australia. Eventually, on the evening of the 16th we had to put on the engine again, just to run it and charge the batteries.

The next night, whilst I was on the midnight to 4 am watch, I sighted what appeared to be a fishing fleet off to port but on our route. I kept an eye on this as there were a lot of Chinese fishing boats around, and I could not be sure if they were trawling. Even if I had known I would still not have been sure of where the nets might be. Worryingly it appeared that they were going to interfere with our course, but eventually it dawned on me that I was looking at Rodriguez Island! Things can be very deceptive at night when you're tired and anyway the shore lights appeared as correct navigation lights. At this stage we were motor-sailing again and would do so for the rest of that night.

The next couple of days and nights there was a good amount of shipping around, mainly visible on the AIS. The ships were no problem to deal with as the AIS gives so much information on course, speed, etc. We contacted any that would get too close according to the AIS and arranged for them to alter course away from us. As a sailing vessel we have the right of way according to the rules for avoiding collision at sea. This was great in theory but in practice can be a bit dodgy as a few hundred thousand tons of steel and cargo take some manoeuvring!

The days were clear and warm with fluffy white trade wind clouds so typical of the conditions and the nights were starry with a full moon too, almost as bright as day. Again we had the steady Trade Winds and minimal sail handling, blissful conditions. Garry caught one fish, a Spanish Mackrel that was promptly served up as Ceviche and Sushi, with the balance fried up as fillets.

On the evening of the penultimate day, we began to motor-sail again, and in the morning, we spotted Mauritius coming up on the horizon, a welcome sight indeed. By 2 pm on 19 October we were securely tied alongside a quay wall in Port Louis, checked in and glad to be ashore.

Before being allowed on shore though we had to wash our footwear in disinfectant trays every time. I'm pretty sure that wasn't good for the shoes. We were to stay here for over a week before moving on to La Reunion Island about 24 hours away.

Port Louis has a strange tidal bore that comes in at random intervals. It's not very big but, if you're on board, you know when it's happened as the boat gets rocked around briefly and strongly.

Mauritius is an independent island, having been governed by both the British and the French in the past, but French speaking mostly. However, driving is on the left-hand side of the road. It has French style cafes and restaurants and the French navy uses Port Louis for maintenance and repairs to its vessels in this ocean.

We could see several Chinese fishing trawlers, happily rusting on their anchors in the middle of the entrance fairway, apparently having been seized for illegal fishing, with some of them listing due to the water inside. It appeared that they had been there a long time.

We made good use of the shoreside eating and drinking facilities! We also went on a tour or two of this lovely island. It was strange to see the English road signs on such a French Island.

Driving on the left-hand side of the road, Mauritius - 26 October 2016

Dawn and Garry made use of the time to go diving several times to the north of Port Louis and at Flic en Flac. Fresh baguettes are readily available with government subsidies, something to be treasured in the mornings, with butter and jam.

Whilst we were all tied up to the quayside Garry spent some time helping *Katerina* to measure up for new sails, as their existing ones were a bit baggy. Dawn and I spent time on board helping Guinilla reduce their food and drinks levels. We also spent a couple of evenings in a nearby hotel, checking out the food and drink menus.

Mauritius to La Reunion

On the afternoon of 27 October the fleet moved out, with all due paperwork done for the short trip across to La Reunion. This is a separate island so not only did we all have to check in again, but we also had to be very careful of what foodstuffs we had on board. Customs were particularly anxious not to allow anything onto the island that might introduce foot and mouth disease.

La Reunion is French, and proud of it too. For a price, most things French are available in the shops and stores. We had a peaceful overnight sail all the way to Port Ouest where the fleet tied up to a fairly rough commercial quayside. There were some power points available to use and we shared one with *Golden Dragon*, another Australian Jeanneau that had joined the fleet in Cocos (Keeling) having sailed from northern Indonesia. He was rafted up on our outside, with *Into the Blue* right behind us. In its earlier life this boat had been nicknamed *Out of the Red.*

This harbour is quite a distance from the nearest town and has no food shops. It did, however, have a sailmaker, a workshop and an outboard/boat sales shop on site. I dropped the outboard in for a service and one of the other boats had all his sails serviced as well. Also there is a local restaurant and dive shop at the shore end of the quay wall.

I had several repairs and services to do on board and so got stuck into them. I had noticed that the cockpit VHF was not operating properly so one of the guys on *Golden Dragon* had a look at it whilst we were all sharing nibbles and drinks in the cockpit. He managed to get it operational but it needed parts that were not available on the island.

Dawn and Garry went off exploring whilst I was working and had a great time. Eventually I joined them and we went off in a rented car to the southern end of the island and to a very upmarket hotel. Dawn and Garry went diving whilst I put my feet up and drank coffee, no diving for me as

I didn't feel 100% that day. We had a good time looking around the west side too. Being French the driving is on the right-hand side of the road.

Although it doesn't appear so on the maps, this is a surprisingly large island with a decent population living here permanently, and a large increase when the tourists arrive from Europe to escape winter.

Halloween was celebrated with a party and fancy dress and was very much enjoyed in the local restaurant, situated next to the dive shop at the shore end of the quay wall. Almost everyone made an effort to dress up and some were unrecognisable in their outfits.

Halloween on Mauritius - myself with Dawn and Garry Cleaver

Eventually, on 4 November, the entire fleet departed this beautiful island heading for Richards Bay in the NE corner of South Africa, still 1,500 miles away. This leg would take us well south of Madagascar to avoid the permanently poor sea conditions, and would last for eight days. Richards Bay is just north of Durban and is close to several game reserves, as well as being a very welcoming port with a couple of marinas.

Having passed through the start gate at 9.00 am we set all plain sail, turned off the engine and sailed away on the deep blue sea. Our course was to take us well south of Madagascar, about 150 to 200 miles south. The reason for this is weather and sea conditions, both of which are always bad due to the large and high land mass of Madagascar, combined with the Agulhas current which is exceptionally strong as it flows south between Africa and Madagascar.

For the first day and a half the sea was quite lumpy and rolly but we made good progress under sail. We encountered several cargo ships passing in our vicinity including one who altered course after I radioed him to enquire about his course intentions. We had no problems sailing all the time until around 2am on the 8th when the wind just vanished for 3 or 4 hours, returning at daybreak again. We were running at about 7-8 knots in winds around force 4-5 north easterly before the breeze backed to the SE direction, all good.

At this stage the generator was very sick. I had found water in the fuel filter in La Reunion but could not find the source. As a result, we were using the main engine for charging. Eventually I got some life out of the genset but I'm sure the fuel system has been terminally damaged by water in the fuel, another job to be done in South Africa.

We continued to sail until late night on the 10th. All this sailing was wonderful and saved a lot of fuel too, so much more pleasant than having the engine running constantly. Eventually though the wind dropped too low and we were forced to use the engine as we had received a weather forecast warning us about a strong low driving north from the southern tip of South Africa and due to reach the coast ahead, so now we had a deadline to get into shelter before it arrived at Richards Bay.

These southerly lows are quite violent and are notorious in the marine world. The winds generated by the low pressure blow against the strong south flowing Agulhas current. This can lead to huge and extremely dangerous seas, not what we wanted! Whole ships have vanished in these stormy conditions.

Initially we motor-sailed but the wind soon picked up again. We took advantage of the weather lull to top up the fuel tank from the jerrycans we carried. Then off with the engine again and we carried on sailing.

The weather conditions had changed and had cooled down noticeably with frequent rain showers too. Now the wind backed around from the Easterly direction to NE and gradually gained strength until we had a force 8 for a few hours on the 12 November. However, as we approached the coast it dropped down to a 5, and then when we got into the port area it dropped out to almost nothing.

Just before we entered the port a Chinese freighter came up behind us at a fair speed. On enquiring on the VHF (Very High Frequency) radio the officer of the watch said the ship would pass ahead of us and changed course to suit. However, as we watched, the ship abruptly changed direction and passed astern of us. I'm sure there were words exchanged on the bridge!

As the channel into the Zululand Yacht Club is quite narrow with shallows on each side we were met and led into the marina by a launch with the WARC officials on board. On arrival we were faced with the challenge of a fairly long boat getting into a short berth in a narrow fairway. All went well for once in front of a crowd of interested fellow sailors and we were welcomed to South Africa by club staff with a bottle of bubbly. We also drank the French champagne that Garry had purchased in La Reunion before departure.

It was great to have crossed the Indian Ocean safely and in relatively benign conditions. Out of the five oceans in the world, this was the last one that I had not sailed on, another bonus. During our stay the WARC and the Ocean Cruising Club (OCC) both organised BBQs, called braies here and I spoke to John and Jenny from the OCC. They are the grandparents of my next crew, joining in Cape Town. I arranged with John for him to join us in Port Elizabeth and sail with us to Cape Town. This enabled him to be happy with the boat and crew for the children on the next leg.

We stayed at the wonderful yacht club for eight days, having a ball and doing some minor work. I had a new filtration system fitted to the generator but still could not get it running properly.

Thanks to the hopeless currency here we found South Africa very cheap and excellent value. On first checking out the club bar, Garry ordered a rum and coke and two beers. When he offered his credit card he was informed that he had not reached the minimum charge and to get another rum! This turned out to total just over $5. Later on I went to get some wine for dinner and was told to go and see which one I wanted for dinner, they all turned out to be Rand 69, or approximately $7.

In our time at the yacht club, we took several trips by four wheel drive to game parks and to the nearest shopping mall. All very civilised and I will certainly return there one day. I bought a phone as well with a local SIM card so as to be in contact with home. It turned out later that this phone would not work in Australia due to some frequency differences

Richards Bay to Port Elizabeth

Eventually we felt we had to move on to Cape Town travelling around the bottom tip of Africa, called Cape Agulhas, not Cape Town which is actually on the western side in the Atlantic Ocean. We found a weather window in the forecasts and set off for Port Elizabeth on 20 November. This was about 400 miles and took just over two days. We were promised a strong south flowing current of up to 6 knots, though all we got was about 2. There were no complaints about this as that's 50 miles a day free travel!

Conditions were so good that we sailed most of it without the engine, other than for charging as the generator was now dead. We had dolphins for company once more and they were a very welcome distraction.

On the way the mainsail roller reefing line decided to take a holiday. It wraps around a drum on the front of the mast and is retained by a simple knot. This knot had undone itself. It was easily reknotted and rewound onto the drum, I just had to make sure that it was rolled on in the correct direction.

On the 22nd we had a hitchhiker on board, a small but very cheeky bird on the foredeck. He stayed with us for a few hours, cleaning and resting, as well as leaving calling cards on the deck. That evening we pulled into Port Elizabeth and tied up to a fairly rough concrete quay wall, having passed by a dodgy looking and rather old marina, with boats secured to it of a similar description!

Port Elizabeth to Cape Town

We spent an awful night there, breaking mooring lines one after another due to the incessant swell rubbing the ropes on the concrete. The barge board that I had bought in Eden paid for itself that night, protecting both the boat and the fenders.

Next morning, we were moved to the rickety marina. This was not a straight forward manoeuvre as the strong wind was on the beam and holding us firmly onto the quayside. After several valiant efforts to get away from the wall we ended up tying off a rope to a point on the other side of what appeared to be a launching ramp and then winching ourselves free. Although the marina looked to be years old, it had apparently been rebuilt after a storm only five years before. *BlueFlyer*, despite being well secured, managed to hit off the walkway in the swell and strong wind causing slight damage to the transom. To make everything worse the main product through this port is manganese oxide ore. This is a fine black powder that coats everything that it contacts, especially boats! Everything on the boat turned black in no time. As soon as the wind changed direction though we washed off as much of this crap as possible but not too successfully. It would take several cleaning operations later in Cape Town to get the decks back to normal. All the boats on the marina had two tone masts, one side black and the other alloy coloured!

John Franklin joined us as arranged and we left this awful place behind us on the morning of 25 November, not a moment too soon. First of all though we had to refuel. We soon found out that there was no fuel dock for small craft in this busy commercial/fishing port, so, after some enquiries, we found out that the refuelling would have to be done at the commercial fishing dock. I was unwilling to move *BlueFlyer* from the marina, so we filled the main tank from the gerrycans and then got a lift in a ute over to the fuel pumps. There we waited for some time until the diesel pump was free. We soon had full cans again and loaded them into the ute again for the trip back. At this point I found out that payment had to be cash or account, not by card. A quick searching of wallets produced the cash, but when I offered it to the manager I was quickly told to put it away and to come into the office, out of sight. He was afraid of being mugged with all that cash. I still wonder how much cash went through the books and how much into his pocket!

I had planned to anchor a couple of times on the way to Cape Town, but the conditions were so good that we just kept going, so as not to waste this opportunity. Winds were very light and the seas flat so it was motor-sailing again. Clear and starry nights with warm days, ideal really to round Cape Agulhas, the southern most point of Africa, and then on into the cold Atlantic Ocean and Cape Town covered in fog! After passing Cape Agulhas we were back in the South Atlantic Ocean. The last time had been in 2007 but that was in the North Atlantic. It didn't feel any different crossing from one ocean to the next but the sea temperature was distinctly cooler than we had become accustomed to, we had lost the warm Aghullas current on rounding the cape.

We approached Cape Town in the dark, having negotiated our way through several hours of heavy fog. As we got closer the fog disappeared and so we were all able to admire the shoreside lights that looked like volcanic lava flowing down the hills around the bay.

We tied up on the V and A marina in the inner harbour at midnight on the 27th, having negotiated two opening bridges in the dark on the way in. There was a welcoming group of WARC boats to help us tie up, happily accepted by us.

Cape Town - 28 November 2016

Cape Town

On our arrival in Cape Town we set to servicing and repair jobs on board, as well as exploring this city and some of the surrounding areas. First up was servicing the ever-faithful Yanmar engine. This now had just over 3,000 hours of use on it, and, other than replacing an impeller in Melbourne and one at sea, has never missed a beat in almost 12 years, thank you Yanmar for such a reliable product. 3,000 hours is approximately equivalent to 150,000+ kilometres on a car!

Next was getting the genoa away for some small repairs to the foot where it had been rubbing on the pulpit, nothing major but Garry still had to be hauled up the forestay to realign the foil sections that the front of the sail slides into and secure all the grub screws before we could drop the sail.

Through the WARC organisers I got a couple of local companies involved. One replaced the mirror in the aft heads with a Perspex one instead of glass. The original had unfortunately fallen out of its clips on the way here and smashed, just missing Dawn's foot. This lack of a mirror may have been a blessing in disguise for Dawn and Garry after the recent trip.

The other engineering company came out to the boat and removed the two unit injectors from the generator. Unit injectors are both the high pressure fuel pump and injector combined into one piece, usually this system is called common rail diesel.

They took them away for repairs and servicing. However, it appeared that these were of such a new design from Bosch that nobody had the necessary equipment to do anything, despite Volkswagen also using them. The result was that two new ones had to be ordered from Germany at considerable cost and, as it turned out, considerable delay as well. South African post is very slow, Customs are very slow and then there were the Christmas and New Year holidays too.

I also arranged some small repairs to the hull and a clean up of the topsides.

Having been chatting with *Into the Blue* about their bunking arrangements, we arranged that two of their crew would stay on the boat over Christmas whilst I was away. Their boat had more crew than sleeping quarters so it was a blessing for them. Thank you, Tom and Dearbhla, they were great boat minders.

I had a long chat with the WARC organisers with regard to leaving the boat here, which was not a problem, and going home for a year out with a view to rejoining in 12 months as I was feeling very down, missing Val. In the end all three of us went home for the Christmas break, Dawn and Garry permanently, and I to return on New Year's Eve. I had a chat with Fiona before deciding about leaving the boat in Cape Town, but in the end, we decided it would be good for me to carry on with the voyage.

Before we left the boat, we rented a car and went through the Stellenbosch wine district, starting with a magnificent private motor museum. We then carried on to a nature reserve cum animal sanctuary further on up in the hills.

There we stayed in lovely bungalows and had two great safaris, one in the afternoon and one the following morning. We were driven around in a party of eight in converted Land Rovers and got to within a couple of metres of a pack of lions, they ignored us totally!

Then we moved on to another animal sanctuary. This is a patrolled area to prevent poaching. However, the first thing we saw were two beheaded white rhinos with the horns cut off. Poachers, usually armed with AK 47 rifles kill the animals and then hack off the horns for sale to the Chinese market.

Just under a nearby tree was a lion dozing in the warmth having had a feed from the carcasses. Further away was a black leopard awaiting his turn to feed. There is a major road running through the reserve so it's very easy for the poachers to operate here. Also on this reserve were cheetah and other wild species. These were kept in big enclosures and were part of an international breeding and conservation programme.

On the way back to the boat we called in to a winery with which I had been in touch from Melbourne prior to departure. The sales manager wanted my old desalination plant so we sat down with her to discuss this, whilst having a tasting session. The samples for tasting were full size measures! I would sip a little and pass them on to Garry. He of course had his own to taste as well! I was driving and so was very abstemious.

Eventually Michelle and I agreed to swap the desalinator for some unspecified amount of their produce. As the winery exports widely, Michelle arranged all the transport. I would box up the desalinator, with its spare parts and manual, over Christmas and leave it ready for collection after my return to the boat.

She also insisted on putting a dozen mixed bottles in the boot of the car for consumption on board. All the arrangements went well and there were 72 mixed bottles of wine delivered to the house whilst I was sailing to the Caribbean.

Later on we all went off to Robbin Island for a tour. This is where the prison that held Nelson Mandela is situated. The trip across is generally wet and rough, taking about 30 minutes. There are full-time guides there waiting to show visitors around. These guides are all ex-inmates and very knowledgeable. We saw the cell where Nelson Mandela was incarcerated for 27 years. We were all amazed at the diet that everyone was fed, every day. This was pinned up on the walls and was not overly generous. After the tour we all had a quick look at the rest of the island, which is quite big and has a permanent population living on it.

Of course, we had to go up to the summit of the world famous Table Mountain by the cable car. The cabins have a revolving floor so that everyone gets to see the views. We were extremely lucky with the weather, it was clear and sunny with the table visible almost the whole time we were in Cape Town, very unusual apparently.

The three of us flew back to Melbourne for Christmas, separately unfortunately. John Franklin left us here to re-join his family.

Dawn and Garry had been on board for three months and some 5,000 miles, and had been the best crew and even better company. However, this was not the last that *BlueFlyer* would see of them.

Driving to the Stellenbosch district north east of CapeTown - 1 December 2016

Chapter 6 -
Cape Town to Brazil

14 January - 2 March 2017
Jamie, Michael and Michael on board

Cape Town to St Helena

On my return during the afternoon of New Year's Eve Michael B. from Seattle was there too having just arrived. Tom and Dearbhla had vacated *BlueFlyer* that morning, leaving a very nice handmade card. They were good guests to have. Michael and I attended the inevitable dock party that evening to welcome in the New Year.

The next day Michael looked around the boat as it had been eight years since he and his wife Suzan had sailed some of the east coast of Australia with us, and then he went away to look around Cape Town on his own. I went off on my own into a suburb of the city and had a tattoo on my left ankle of a *Blue Flyer* kangaroo in memory of Val.

The majority of the rally fleet set off on 7 Januay 2017, heading to St Helena, with one or two going to Namibia on the way. *BlueFlyer* and two other boats were left behind with ongoing repairs and waiting for parts.

Another Michael and his girlfriend Jamie came aboard for a visit. They were crewing the next leg to Brazil. They dropped off some of their luggage. Jamie being the granddaughter of John Franklin. When I saw how much luggage they had I did wonder where it would all fit! As everyone was on board, I took us all out into the bay for a quick sail.

It was just as well I did so as I found several ball bearings on deck. I knew immediately what had happened. There is a sliding cage, called a car, that controls the sheet that controls the mainsail and this had broken at one end releasing the balls. Fortunately, the local sailmaker had new ends and kits in stock. He brought them to the boat for me. Now when this happened before in Melbourne the cabin ceiling panels and wood beams had to be stripped out to get to the track retaining bolts so as to be able to replace the car, taking most of the day. I wasn't going to do this. After consultation with the sailmaker, who didn't like my idea, I cut one of the end retaining pieces in half, stuffed the new balls into the car and then screwed the two end pieces in place, this has lasted to date!

I also serviced the winches and cleaned up generally.

Eventually the new injectors arrived and were fitted. We test ran the generator satisfactorily and were much relieved. As this was going on, I had a diver and her assistant clean the bottom of the hull, it needed doing! Last time I had the hull cleaned was in Melbourne.

We filled up with diesel, water and food, cleared Customs and Immigration, despite a very obnoxious and obstructive official, and had a final meal on the marina before setting off on Saturday 14 January. There was one other rally boat still there, and when he left he went straight up to the Azores and on to the Mediterranean.

Michael B. is a sailor from Seattle with much experience and had been sailing on *BlueFlyer* before. Michael and Jamie were both inexperienced novices, having attended a day sailing course in South Africa. They were both in their late teens and seemed terribly young to me, but I dare say I was very old to them. Jamie had long dark hair that shed alarmingly all over the boat. I was still finding it 18 months after their departure.

I had planned an early start, 7.00 am, and we left the dock a little before that. However, the bridge operator had gone absent so we were left stooging around the area, waiting. I called the Port Controller eventually. I don't know what he did, but the bridge was opened in a few minutes and then we were away. There were various suggestions made as to the operator's whereabouts but I think he was just ignoring us.

Once out of the harbour area we quickly put up the sails and knocked off the engine. There was a good southerly breeze and a 2 metre swell running.

Jamie and Michael did not appreciate this motion so I sent them below to sleep for a while. This turned into two days before I got fed up and told them to get up on deck as the other Michael and I were tired from doing watch on watch every three hours.

We were enjoying the fresh conditions and the boat was cruising under sail at 7-8 knots. The wind was SSW and a force 4, 15-20 knots on the beam. We were heading for St Helena, an island in the middle of the south Atlantic that is only reachable by boat. Its only claim to fame is that this is where Napoleon Buonaparte was exiled by the British and where he died.

On the second day the wind gradually increased and so I put a reef in the mainsail. It also backed around to SSE and so more behind us. That meant we started rolling about 20 degrees each side. This motion would stay with us all the way to St Helena. Not at all pleasant for anyone who wasn't feeling too good. Jamie, unfortunately, never felt really good the whole voyage, but young Michael settled down well. So much so that there was never any unfinished food left. Teenage males can eat their own weight in provisions every day!

As the crew settled in I started a proper watch system going, three hours on and nine hours off so that everyone got a good sleep. Activity consisted of watching and reading as "Otto" did all the steering. "Otto" was the Raymarine auto pilot and was a godsend as standing and steering any boat for three hours at a stretch is very tiring.

Towards the evening on that second day the wind kept rising, eventually gusting 38-40 knots so we rolled in more main and reefed in the genoa. It was midnight before the breeze started to ease. It was a cool night and we had several waves splash into the cockpit.

By the time the dawn came the wind had dropped and the sea state was settling so we opened out the genoa and put the spinnaker pole on it to hold the sail steady and stop it flapping all the time. We were cruising along at around 7 knots, on course and a bit quicker than expected.

These conditions kept up so we rolled away the mainsail and sailed on under the poled-out genoa only. This meant the mainsail could not gybe us accidentally, a dangerous and potentially damaging manoeuvre.

It was great having a silent engine and the generator running well again. We used it to charge up the batteries as it's more fuel efficient and quieter than the engine.

All good things come to an end and during the dawn watch the wind died away so we had to motor-sail again for a few hours. Later on that day we put the main back up in the lightish breezes. However, the engine had to be used on and off pretty much all the rest of the way. The winds remained light and very much behind us. The conditions remained good, though warm and humid.

We were all feeling good and eating well. I made sure everyone was drinking plenty of water too. We had stocked up with bottled water in Cape Town before leaving. The boat's tank water was being used for the occasional showers and for cooking.

During the day on the 24th we put six jerrycans of diesel into the main engine tank, the engine having been used for much more time than I had hoped.

In the dark of early morning of 25 January we spotted lights ahead and then when the sun rose there was St Helena, just where it was supposed to be! By 11.00 am we were tied to a mooring in the Jamestown Bay area, along with most of the rally fleet. As a boat can stay here free of charge for only three days we were going to be one of the few boats remaining shortly. We watched most of them sail away the next day, having had their three day stay.

On arrival at St Helena the first thing you meet, after mooring, are the water taxis. These are the only way in as the constant swell means that if you go in by dinghy someone has to take it back to the boat, otherwise it will be destroyed. It's easier just to pay the fare.

Landing here is interesting! You arrive at the landing platform on your taxi. This is a grand name for a concrete step that has a rope hanging down to grab for stability as you launch yourself onto the sea water covered slab. It's not always wet as sometimes the swell wave doesn't reach quite high enough! There are different levels to use depending on the tide. In any case it's not unusual to get your feet wet, if nothing else.

After landing safely the first stop is at the "yacht club". There are no yachts based here so it's only for visitors. It's about 30 metres up from the landing area. It has a toilet and some chairs and tables, but that's about it. The building is original and somewhat rough and ready.

Having made your number there you receive directions to customs about 100 metres away. In you go and present passports, etc, fill out forms and then you're free to go and find the police station, which handles immigration. It's in the town and is about a 10 minute walk.

There is only one town, Jamestown. It's not very big and has the only bank on the island. There's no ATM anywhere and everyone gets paid by cheque on Friday. The internet is only available at one of the nearby bars. It's both slow, by satellite, and expensive. The bar in question was run by an English girl who sailed here with her boyfriend, who was also working on the island. We spent a lot of time in this bar, eating, drinking and attempting to connect to the internet.

Jamie and Michael took a look at Jacobs Ladder. This is the short cut to the top of the hill where the old fort was built by the British. Standing up here gives fantastic views out to sea and over the town. It's a 688 step climb at 41 degree slope, not so easy. Michael B and I went the long way and met them at the top. We arrived first!

We arranged a taxi ride the next day and went off to Napoleon's house. It has been restored and would not have been a bad place to be exiled, with his staff and his servants to look after him. After his death Napoleon was buried on the island, but the French requested his return and now he is interred in Paris. Jamie and Michael had a look at a fenced in concrete slab in the middle of a field. This was his grave, we were told.

We also headed south to look at the brand new airport, built at vast expense by the British government. It was reported in the press to be unusable due to wind shear affecting all incoming planes bigger than small twin engine jets. It has since opened for smaller commercial planes that give a regular service from Cape Town at great cost, being a monopoly. There is a new road to the airport from the town and it appeared to be the only decent road on the island. We also visited the governor's residence, a very nice 18th century mansion with a tortoise in the garden reputed to be around 150 years old.

Everything on St Helena has to come in by ship from Cape Town at quite a cost, so nothing is cheap here. The supply cum passenger ship had been sold as a ferry to somewhere in Scotland the previous year and then had to be returned under charter when the airport couldn't open!

The island is quite small, but attractive. It has a temperate climate with plenty of rain and so is a lush green colour. The population is just under 5,000 permanent residents, mainly of British descent and all with government jobs, either directly or indirectly. There are no indigenous industries here, other than small farming, tourism and fish.

On the last day we went swimming with whale sharks which love this area. These are the biggest sharks in the world, but are absolutely harmless to humans. They don't have teeth but are baleens and sieve their food out of the water.

St Helena to Cabadelo

Before leaving St Helena I filled up all the empty jerrycans, bringing them to and from the boat by taxi, having topped up the boat fuel tanks and ran the desalination plant again to top up the water.

We let go of the mooring late afternoon on 27 January and headed to Brazil, initially to Salvador and the big carnival celebrations that are held there, and where the WARC were preparing to greet the fleet.

The winds were SE to ESE and force 3-4, so really pleasant conditions, bar of course the rolling. This is always present when running with the wind, there is just no escaping it.

Having discussed our course and destination options, remember we were late leaving Cape Town, we decided to go directly to Cabadelo on the NE corner of Brazil. This shortened our leg by a couple of hundred miles and cut out the upwind leg from Salvador to Cabadelo. It turned out that another boat in the rally was doing the same thing.

We barely used the engine in these conditions for almost 10 days! We had definitely reverted to being a sailing boat again. We even had the big lightweight gennaker flying again for several days in a row! Then we replaced it with the genoa. Young Michael and I tried using the gennaker as a spinnaker, it was not designed for this but it did sort of work. The only problem was getting the sail back down, it really wanted to stay up. After a lot of effort and talking severely to it, we eventually retrieved the sail and resolved never to try that manoeuvre again!

All this time sailing along we were doing around 5-6 knots and having a great time. Jamie's stomach had more or less settled down, young Michael had turned out to be a good cook too, once we stopped him emptying the salt into everything! They are both lifeguards at home as well as being Eagle Scouts and are well used to being on the water, just not sailing.

We were having the occasional rain shower, but nothing heavy, and the sky was gradually becoming overcast but the wind was steady and we were just cruising along very happily.

We all sat down one afternoon and started drawing up the repairs/ maintenance list for Brazil. There wasn't too much on it and, for something to do, we did some of the work as we were sailing along.

I fixed the loose retaining bolt on the cooker, and cleaned the floor under it whilst I was there. It badly needed the clean-up.

Michael and Jamie got stuck into the draining locker. This is a top loading one next to the sinks. After they had taken everything out, and ditched the rotten eggs that were in it, they cleaned up and dried it, before refilling it with provisions.

Michael B and I removed the faulty hand operated bilge pump in the cockpit. The retaining ring for the diaphragm had broken so it was no longer pumping. Michael glued the plastic ring together and I refitted it with a double worm drive clip to reinforce the glue. Once it was all back in place and working again we were happy campers. It's still working.

So January turned into February with little activity. We put a couple of jerrycans of fuel into the generator tank up forward. On the 6th we ran with the engine as the breeze had slackened off somewhat, and we were all looking forward to land again! This burst of motor-sailing lasted for three days and made up for all the sailing we had done.

Michael B. reported to me that he had overextended his knee and was fairly certain he had torn his meniscus again. A repeat of a similar accident many years before. He was now planning to leave us in Cabadelo to fly home to Seattle and have the knee surgically attended to there, very unfortunate for him. This was the only injury on the whole trip, the medical kit was barely touched other than for plasters.

On the 9th, within a hundred miles of Cabadelo, we stopped the boat, there was little wind anyway Jamie and Michael jumped over for a cooling swim, there being no sharks or crocodiles visible. As soon as they were back on board, we put out the genoa again, the breeze having increased and we were off sailing once more. I rolled in half the sail after a while as we were going too fast for our planned arrival! It was necessary to arrive as the tide was rising in the river, otherwise you can get well and truly stuck in the muddy banks.

We arrived at the river mouth on 10 February as I had planned, the tide was right and so away with the sails and we motored the 7 miles upstream to Jacaré Marina to await the rest of the fleet, and carry out the boat maintenance. The marina was distinctly home built but welcome all the same. Mooring on it was Mediterranean style, stern to with bow lines on moorings holding us steady.

As soon as we arrived the marina owner, a charming Frenchman, brought me to the nearest town to check in. He warned me on the way that this would take some time as one of the officials would sit in his office for up to an hour leaving the new arrival to sit outside whilst he had his coffee! Anyway I eventually got us all cleared in.

Michael B. wasted no time in heading home, via about four flights. He arrived safely and his knee has been repaired. Unfortunately, before his departure, Michael managed to trip on the walkway, not surprising really as it was patched together with old pallets. He cut his head open and banged his knee as well, and then, later, he overbalanced in the cockpit too. This time he gave his arm a good bang, it was sore!

As Michael and Jamie's money had all but run out, we three sat down to discuss the future and what they wanted to do. After some chat they both said that they would like to stay on board as they could not foresee any way that they would get the opportunity to travel to the Caribbean again in the future. The main reason being that the Rand was such a weak currency. I suggested then that they stay on until Panama and I would feed them. I was very happy to do this as it saved me having to find more crew in Brazil. Up to now we had all shared the costs of fuel, food and fees equally. The new arrangement was agreed there and then, and it worked out well.

We were going to spend nearly three weeks here until the official start of the final leg up to St Lucia, which would be the end of the rally. Jacaré village took about 15 minutes to explore, Jacaré apparently means crocodile in Portuguese, but there aren't any here now. It's a dirt-poor fishing village and is about as far from any city as you can get. It does however have a train service with the station about a 10 minute walk from the marina. The fares are ridiculously cheap, about 10 cents to the nearest town, actually I think it's a flat rate to anywhere in the province.

We spent some days in the village, having found a private house that opens for lunch each day. There was no menu, just whatever the housewife happened to be cooking that day. It was cheap to us, and good food. The locals ate there too and were all friendly even though we had no Portuguese and they had no English.

This was a very peaceful spot to have the boat moored. However, one afternoon, as we were all on the boat, a wave came in and set all the boats violently rocking. There was suddenly a loud bang on the boat. When we checked we found one of the safety line stanchions had broken due to our neighbour's boat hitting it with their deck. I managed to remove the stanchion by dropping the roof lining in the saloon and found that the bolt that goes through the deck had snapped off. I brought it to the marina people who were French and spoke some English. They got it to the local machine shop. There they drilled out the remains of the base bolt and welded in a new bolt, problem solved!

Another day we went off to the nearby town and looked around, had an evening meal and generally had a good time. As well as that we found that you could walk along the beach to a neighbouring village which had a cafe/restaurant in a very big tree. It was called, oddly enough in English, the Tree House. Once a week there was a biggish market held in the same village, and a smaller version each day. Needless to say we did some souvenir shopping and generally poked around.

We also spent time in a nearby town which had a large church or cathedral, I don't know the difference. This was a beautiful building complete with a tour guide. We, and several other tourists, took a tour. However, as it was all in Portuguese, we had to make up our own commentary, I don't think it bore any resemblance to the official one, but was probably a lot more fun.

Another day we went to the chief town of the area called Olinda by minibus to see the local carnival. It was amazingly good, with huge crowds and many really colourful floats that took hours to pass by. Apparently, there are several versions of Carnival in Brazil, depending on where you happen to be. The transport was organised by the WARC people and was very efficient and quick in mini buses. However three of the boat captains were robbed of money and cameras during the celebrations.

Local church near marina - 16 February 2017

Carnival decorations in Olinda - 18 February 2017

In between these activities I was servicing the engine and generator, arranging for fuel, keeping the water tanks full and generally doing maintenance in the mornings before the temperature and humidity got too high. I had the air con running whenever the electricity was on which was great comfort. The main fuse for the marina had a habit of tripping and, because the village was at the end of the power line, the voltage varied between 150 to 250 volts! The lower end would trip out the air con, but when it was running it was great.

We all spent a lot of time on the internet and eating in the marina cafe, as well as partying in the evenings as the other boats arrived.

Eventually the time came to do the final food run. The WARC laid on a minibus or two to the nearest shopping mall. This had a Carrefour supermarket, part of an international chain of large supermarkets, which did well out of all the boats. Thank goodness they accepted credit cards. I bought a vacuum cleaner, soon named ET, as well as food, etc. The three of us ate lunch there in a fast-food outlet, all in Portuguese.

Once again, we all went to town to check out with the same guy that had checked us in. It took hours for him to process everyone, but eventually it was all done. Then it was downtown to customs for their clearance located in the docks area. No problems or delays there.

We all enjoyed our time here, especially the carnival, but agreed that we would not be returning to Brazil in the foreseeable future. The consensus being that it was a third world country with first world pricing, not to mention all the crime.

Chapter 7 - Brazil to St Lucia

2 March - 16 April 2017
Jamie and Michael on board

Cabadelo to Grenada, Port Louis

Our next leg was to be non-stop across the north of Brazil and into the Caribbean to Grenada.

At the pre-start briefing the WARC gave us all a waypoint near Grenada which we had to stay north of to avoid possible piracy problems from Trinidad. This was more a precaution than anything else, or so we all hoped!

This leg of the trip was approximately 1,900 miles in length and about 12 days duration in theory. My plan, with the weather router's advice, was to go well offshore to the north so as to miss the counter current from the Amazon River. Others were going well inshore to visit some islands near the coast along the way and at least one boat was planning to watch an Ariane rocket lift off at dawn from French Guiana.

We left the dock at 7.20 am on the morning of 2 March and motored downriver to the Atlantic Ocean once more. The start line was crossed at 8.25 am and we were away again in company with several other rally boats.

In the drizzle we put up full sails and turned off the engine, the wind was SE and around 15-20 knots, the Trade Winds again, hopefully. The engine was rested till late the next day, with any luck a sign of good sailing to come. The drizzle developed into proper rain, though the sailing remained good. The night of the 4th we had some dolphins, as well as lots of lightning around. Michael put all the hand-held electronics into the microwave for protection, the theory being that the oven will act as a Faraday cage and will divert the electricity around the metal box. We never found out, thank goodness, if this does give protection from a lightning strike. Later on the sky cleared and the stars came out and there's an awful lot of them when you look from offshore with no background light.

The follwing day the wind backed to the NE so we altered the boat's course to keep a favourable wind angle. Eventually the breeze faded away and so finally the engine had to go back on.

We were approaching the equator, an area that is the equivalent of the doldrums on the eastern side of the ocean, at this stage and that is why the low wind and change of direction. The doldrums are much narrower on this side of the ocean and we motor-sailed through this area of little wind in about 36 hours and then stopped the engine again. Whilst I had the generator running, we also had the air conditioner going. The saloon became very popular in the cooler temperature of 22 degrees, and the humidity was also reduced from around 90% to only 55%. What a difference that made.

The boat crossed the equator again, for the third time at 5.30 pm on 5 March. This was Michael and Jamie's first time so, of course, there was a small ceremony involving shaving cream and alcohol! The alcohol was for Neptune/Poseidon, not for human consumption. They were suddenly and magically changed from Pollywogs to Shellbacks in a flash. Cleaning up took much longer! A celebration that they can never do again as you can only have it the first time you cross the line. Despite keeping a careful watch for it, none of us actually saw the line itself. If you look you will see it's shown on all the maps!

There was a lovely dawn to greet us, a reward from Poseidon no doubt. During my normal morning inspection of the boat, I found the port side guard rail had detached itself overnight from the gate. I quickly reinstalled it, not that anyone was going on deck, to prevent any overboard accidents.

Later in the afternoon I eased our course to a more westerly direction, but that didn't stop the heavy rain from coming in on us with winds which were slowly increasing, as was our speed. We put a reef in the main so as to improve our comfort, but that didn't stop the incessant rolling, nothing ever could. At this stage we didn't take much notice of the roll, just put up with it. Our speed was between 6 and 8 knots towards the Caribbean, so all was well and everyone was happy.

On the morning of the 10th we had a busy time. There was seaweed on deck that needed clearing before it dried out, I saw a small hole in the main where it had been touching the mast spreader, so we reefed down the sail until the hole was enclosed within the roller so as to protect the sail, there was a flying fish in the cockpit and I found the galley tap running with water spread everywhere. Fortunately we still had plenty of water in the tanks. It was all go for a while! Despite all this we were still averaging about 6 knots.

Finally, on 12 March the wind started easing a bit even though our speed kept up around 7 knots, helped by the favourable current pushing us along. To brighten up the day and give us a conversation point we had a visitor. A small bird perched on the pulpit for a while, and even though he or she left several calling cards on deck, it was good to have the company. Eventually it flew away, home presumably, and we kept on sailing.

The next couple of days were unremarkable with good boat speed and favourable conditions. There was some shipping around but nothing too close for comfort.

The 15th was a squally sort of day, with winds up to 40+ knots. I hand steered for a while as "Otto", the autopilot, was being overpowered by the waves. They were pushing the boat from side to side and this caused "Otto" to cry enough and then switch off. Eventually I turned him on again as the conditions calmed and normality was restored to *BlueFlyer.* Hand steering a boat for any length of time is quite tiring to do, and anyway the electronic helmsman is much more consistent.

Later in the afternoon the rope that holds the mainsail out along the boom, known as the outhaul, broke. We dropped the sail and secured it to the deck until the conditions eased in the evening. All three of us then manoeuvred the sail back onto the boom, and secured the outhaul. This broke again three times when we hoisted the sail. Eventually I succeeded by using a steel shackle attached to a soft shackle to secure the foot of the sail to the end of the mandrill inside the boom. To do this is not that easy out at sea as someone has to stand on the cockpit table at full stretch whilst the boom is pulled down as far as possible. Then the shackles have to be attached by feel only, whilst pulling the foot of the sail along the boom. The sail rolls up on the stainless-steel tube inside the boom as it is furled.

We then got going again with the reefed main and full genoa. We were all tired after all the struggling with this heavy and awkward sail for so long.

Carefully making sure to stay north of the pirated waypoint, I wonder if they knew not to go north of the point, we finally saw Grenada on the horizon. I was beginning to think that the island had been moved.

After several more hours sailing the south coast of the island, we rounded the western tip and entered Port Louis. We tied up in Port Louis Marina at nearly 11 o'clock that night. We were glad to be in, and slept exceptionally well having been welcomed by several of the fleet who had arrived before us, and, unfortunately, presented us with a couple of bottles of rum punch. I say unfortunately because, starting at about 10.30 am next morning *Golden Dragon* decided to host a rum punch tasting session, that eventually finished around 6 pm whereupon we all retired to a local microbrewery for a BBQ and more tastings. It really can be tough this cruising life!

We ended up staying a week here in this clean and modern marina where everything works, except the ATM on the dock. The WARC fleet kept emptying it of cash, and the bank was very slow refilling it with more cash. Perhaps the people involved could not believe how quickly we could empty it.

Check in was easy, just many forms, all asking the same questions, to be filled in, but no problems. Jamie was concerned all the time about her South African passport, but we never had any problems with it. Michael has both South African and Dutch passports so had no concerns. My Australian one was welcomed everywhere. I kept my Irish one in reserve!

During this stay I managed to get several of the repairs done. The mainsail was removed again by all of us and carried to the local sailmaker. We found a rip across a panel near the mast as well as the small hole seen earlier. On top of that the batten pockets were wearing and an extra patch was put on where the sail had been touching the spreaders. It's a bulky heavy piece of cloth when you are carrying it in warm and humid conditions.

All the winches were serviced and I had the mast and rigging checked over as well by some riggers who were working on a nearby boat. All got a clean bill of health which heartened me for the Pacific crossing that was to come.

Down below I fixed a couple of minor leaks from the deck and mast, just required more mastic in the appropriate places, or should I say I thought I did. I also dropped the sinks out of the counter top and resealed around the upper flanges and then refitted them both, an awkward job but not difficult. The original sealant had begun to disintegrate and looked bad too.

I removed the main bilge pump float switch and reattached it properly, not an easy job as the generator sits on top in the way. The switch had decided to float in the water and so was no longer turning on the pump and so not drying out the bilge sump. We also topped up the water tanks as needed. The last thing we did was refill the fuel tank on the way out. The fuel dock was in an awkward spot on the opposite side of the entrance, not too easy to back into, but no harm done.

In between all this work there were several celebratory parties on the dock and on various boats. One of them was a mass celebration of crossing the equator. This was organised and conducted by a retired Australian navy bosun from *Golden Dragon*. All the people who made the crossing for the first time were converted to "Shellbacks" and certified as well.

Port Louis marina is well worth a visit if you're sailing in the neighbourhood.

Neptune arrives in Grenada - 19 March 2017

A week after our arrival, with all known jobs done, we left Port Louis and travelled a short distance to Dragon Bay, still in Grenada. This bay has an underwater sculpture park that is available for diving. I didn't dive on it but I'm told it's a very interesting sight to see the creations placed under water. It's also a good anchorage to boot.

Next morning we left this bay and headed off to Tyrell Bay in Curaçao, one of the neighbouring islands. Here we found a mooring so that made for a secure and quiet night. For the next week and a half we moved slowly north, visiting about half a dozen bays, swimming, eating, drinking and generally having a relaxing time on board. The Tobago Quays in particular were delightful with turtles everywhere. There was a mooring fee payable to the ranger who was supposed to come round in his boat, but no one appeared so I kept the money. Michael and Jamie would go off meeting others from the rally of their own age, either swimming across or using the dinghy. They had now become much more confident and relaxed and seemed to be having a ball.

The harbour in Bequia - 31 March 2017

After the Quays we tied up in Port Elizabeth in Bequia, another stunning island. Finally, we got to Marigot Bay in St Lucia on 5 April and were given a very convenient berth for the few days there. We had had a wonderful sail north to St Lucia from Bequia, going up the east coast, that is the Atlantic side, which is normally much rougher. Flat seas and trade winds, ideal conditions. It took the whole day, after all it was 60 odd miles.

Marigot Bay is where the English fleet hid from the French fleet back in the 1700s and is extremely well sheltered from any rough seas. It is popular with larger boats too, several super yachts being present.

During our three days here we checked into St Lucia, visited the very upmarket hotel that owns the marina and had a meal in the much overrated and overpriced restaurant called the Rainforest Hideaway on the opposite side of the bay. The staff there flatly refused to serve tap water, only expensive bottled stuff so John, our newest crew member, took our glasses into the women's toilets and filled them from the tap in there, at least that's what we all hoped he did! By this stage we had been joined by John Moffitt from Florida for a few weeks sailing before he flew to his own boat in Latvia. John and Priscilla are a lovely couple Val and I had met in Dublin many years before.

The Pitons of St Lucia - 6 April 2017

On 8 April the fleet departed Marigot Bay, heading to Rodney Bay and the finish of both the rally and my first circumnavigation. We all formed up in size order, nose to tail, and headed off to Rodney Bay, via the capital Castries for a quick in and out of the harbour there.

By 3.00 pm we were all docked and had begun celebrating our arrival, again! Much rum punch disappeared, and much more had to be acquired by the organisers. The was also a nice buffet on the dock for all.

This is where John left us after a much too brief visit. We however were staying here till the 16th to wait for my sister to arrive for a sailing holiday. She was flying in on the 15th from England.

The three of us had a great time in St Lucia, renting a car and driving around the island, refreshing my memories, and Michael and Jamie making new ones. Being an English island driving is on the left as it should be.

There was also much socialising among the boats. This gradually got less and less as boats sailed off into the sunset, all with varying plans for the future. Some headed back to the USA, some back to Europe and some, like us, were going Caribbean cruising.

Eventually my sister Judith joined us, by which time we had the boat ready to leave the following morning. We were the second last one of the fleet to leave.

Chapter 8 - St Lucia to Panama

16 April - 20 June 2017
Jamie, Judith and Michael on board

St Lucia to Martinique

With Judith safely on board, and having had a good night's sleep, we slipped our berth on Sunday 16 April. We had a goodbye blast or two from the last rally boat still in Rodney Bay, *Wishanger 2*. The boys on board had become good friends with Jamie and Michael since Cape Town, along with the crew of *Into the Blue*. They were all of a similar age and kept meeting up duringthe various stopovers along the way. I'm sure they have all said that they'll meet up again in the future, but I think it's unlikely, perhaps they'll stay in touch though.

We had a great time in Rodney Bay and St Lucia in general. This was my second visit, with 10 years in between. The marina had changed hands during this period and tripled in size, becoming much more efficient and spotlessly clean. The restaurants had all improved as had the whole island in general. The island has several advantages for us as English is the major language and driving is on the correct left-hand side.

Now that we were in the Caribbean properly there should be no more long trips, nearly all would be day sailing which would suit everyone, with the next destination in sight before departure most of the time. However most of the Caribbean is made up of independent islands, each with its own check-in, check-out procedures and English is probably in the minority.

On leaving Rodney Bay we turned due north to our next Island, Martinique, a French offshore protectorate, part of the French overseas territory and very well equipped for boaties. It took all of 2 hours to reach Le Marin on the SW corner of the island. We anchored off in St Anne's Bay, next to two other rally boats. This is a sandy bottomed and shallow area, ideal for yachts and powerboats to wait in safety. As soon as we were secured, we launched the dinghy and headed in to the town. I headed into the marina office and checked us all in. This is now done on a computerised system, no paperwork involved.

I also booked a marina berth for the following day as I was planning to stay here a couple of days so that everyone could look around at leisure. Whilst checking in I also half cleared us out, very convenient if you're only going to be a few days in port.

Monday morning, we shifted to our marina berth, but not till there was a bit of 'hoo ha' about where we would be as the staff were running late and boats that should have departed hadn't and boats that should have docked ahead of us couldn't, but in the end all was good. Shore power was promptly connected and the air con was running!

We soon found out that this being Easter all the shops ashore were shut, except for a few restaurants.

On Tuesday I went into Caraibe Marin, one of the chandleries. This was the same place and the same people who had replaced the rudder bearings after the first Atlantic crossing 10 years previously. There I bought enough courtesy flags to get us back to Australia.

Whilst I was in the building I went upstairs to a sailmaker. I had brought one of the rope bags ashore with me to get replacements for both of them, these are small bags in the cockpit that collect up excess ropes. After 12 years they were both very second hand, despite Peter's repairs earlier. I showed him the bag, no problem to make new ones. He then showed me a selection of colours, and we settled on grey and he would have the two of them ready for tomorrow. That evening we dined in the local restaurant, excellent fare as usual.

The next morning, I called in for the bags, which were ready, but only half the size. He explained that there wasn't enough material. I took them anyway and put the new ones on one side of the companionway one above the other and the better of the two old ones on the other side. This would do till I could get proper new ones.

I met up with another WARC participant here for a meal in a restaurant that night. He and his wife had been with us on the very first round the world rally 10 years previously and it was great to chat again. His wife was in Germany and he was with the boat in Guatemala. I can't remember why Gerry was in the neighbourhood, Guatemala is not exactly next door.

The only deadline on this cruise through the Caribbean was in July when I had to fly to Dublin for a memorial service for my wife Val, so no rushing around needed. I planned to catch a plane from Panama City on the Pacific side of the canal to Dublin, and Jamie and Michael would fly home to South Africa from there also.

Martinique to Dominica

From Le Marin we had a 6 hour trip around the SW corner to St Pierre on the NW coast. On this leg we passed by Diamond Rock. This is a rocky island just off the coast that had been occupied and fortified by the British in Nelson's time, much to the anger of France. Eventually the French retook it.

The small town of St Pierre had been devastated by a volcano in the early 20th century. Interestingly one of the few survivors was a prisoner being held in the jail, he was unscathed. If you were to look at the hill above the town you could see where the eruption blew off half the hillside, most of which landed on the town causing utter devastation and great loss of life.

We went ashore in the dinghy, landing on the black sandy beach and then wandered around the town for several hours before having a meal in the square. This was a lovely stopover for a couple of days. I finished our checking out in the Tourist Office, when I found it half way up the hill out of town. This was on a computer connected to one in Le Marin.

Onwards and northwards we went, my favourite island of Dominica being the next visit. This island has been described as Jurassic Park without the dinosaurs! It's pretty much undeveloped tropical rainforests and rivers, with a couple of towns and roads.

We took 5 hours to get to our temporary anchorage at Roseau, the capital, averaging 8 knots in wonderful sailing conditions. As we were anchoring one of the locals approached the boat saying we could not stay there at anchor. Here we stayed only long enough to have dinner on board and a short sleep as next morning we left before dawn for Portsmouth in the NW of the island. I had not visited here before and was looking forward to comparing this town with Roseau. This island has a population of only about 65,000 people and when the cruise liners arrive in Roseau the passengers overwhelm the whole town and the liners completely obliterate the area from the sea!

We were met by Laurence of Arabia. This is the name that Megs, one of the local boatmen, uses. He is one of the well organised group of boatmen here who have arranged amongst themselves that only one boat goes out to greet each visiting boat. It used to be total mayhem as at least half a dozen would crowd around all shouting and calling for any business. He operates as a water taxi cum tourist guide, as well as being a fisherman in the low season. He guided us to the mooring field and stood by while we anchored, and then took me a couple of miles in his boat to the check in office. All the usual paperwork was done in a friendly manner at the police and customs office and then Megs brought me back to the boat.

We arranged for him to collect us all in the morning for a boat ride up the local river. That evening we took the dinghy ashore and looked around before having an excellent dinner in a local restaurant.

Next morning Megs arrived as arranged and off we went in his boat with no idea where we were going. It wasn't a long journey to the local river mouth, but not the most scenic, much runoff being present from the houses and small shoreside industries and workshops. As we entered the river under quite a low bridge the trees were closing in overhead and it became quite gloomy but very 'jungly', with a lot of humidity.

We motored up river for about a mile and then pulled into a backwater with a landing platform. Here we met another boat coming downstream. From now on, Megs explained, no engines are permitted so as to preserve the river banks and also not to frighten any of the local fauna. So out with the oars and Megs had a leisurely row upstream for another hour or so, pausing every so often to point out flora and fauna living in the area.

We soon reached as far as we were able to go and climbed out of the boat onto a pathway on the river bank. A couple of minutes walking and we arrived at a bar! We couldn't believe it was real, so naturally we checked it out with a couple of cold beers to make sure this was real. It was surrounded by the jungle with no other way in or out. Tourist business only I suppose.

As we were chatting to the owner Megs was plaiting some presents for us from stalks growing wild around here. We still have them, mine is a bird on a stick. I did wonder what the Australian customs would make of it. The lady who owns the bar was interesting. She explained that she has a Dominican mother, a Jamaican father, was born in London and worked in New York as an EKG nurse! Extraordinary the people you may meet anywhere. After a couple of drinks, it was back to *BlueFlyer* and our own version of reality. Dinner ashore again. We like to dine ashore so as to spread a little money around, provided it's not too expensive.

Chocolateria in Dominica - 22 April 2017

Dominica to Guadeloupe

We left our anchorage the next day, heading for Guadeloupe further north. It rained most of that day, and was generally miserable with rough seas and a good deal of wind. We had to decide between going to Guadeloupe or the Isles de Saintes, tough choice! As it was a miserable wet day we decided on the bigger island, with me hoping it would be easier navigation on arrival.

About half way across we met up with an open fishing boat with a solo fisherman on board waving and shouting to us. It turned out that he had dropped his GPS into the water in his boat and was now lost! On top of that his outboard was running low on fuel. We towed him for a while and then he went off again toward the Isles de Saintes without a word. I presume he arrived safely but we never heard anything. Considering he had little fuel he went off at great speed.

We headed into a small, and cramped, marina in Terre Basse, on the SW corner of Guadeloupe, getting there at lunch time. In the end we only stayed here for two nights even though the weather forecast seemed to be saying more of this rain for several days.

The main town, called Pointe au Pitre, apparently has several restaurants, all closed that day, so we ate in a small local one, there was no choice as to which one!

On 25 April we'd had enough of this not very welcoming area and headed off north again to Pigeon Island where we anchored for lunch before moving on to Dehaize Bay for the night. This is a lovely looking area so Michael and Jamie went ashore to look around. Judith and I stayed aboard. From here is where we departed from Guadeloupe the next morning and sailed on to Jolly Harbour in Antigua. This is on the north coast where Val and I had spent a Christmas here many years ago, but it had changed a fair bit in the meantime, with a modern marina along with all the facilities needed.

Guadeloupe to Antiqua

I would have gone to one of the other major marinas on the south coast but it was Antigua Race Week and so I didn't even try as they would be full of racing yachts and their crews.

We rented a car and drove south down to English and Falmouth harbours to have a look at all the race boats moored there. There were some really pretty ones as well as the ultra-modern racing machines.

The island is fairly typical of the Caribbean, with poor roads and little money, but still having some very wealthy as well as very poor people. Crime is ever present in St Johns, the capital. At this time Judith heard from home that her daughter was unwell, so she decided to cut short her holiday and fly home.

I had planned to go to St Croix and Puerto Rico for a visit and a looksee but due to the visa requirements necessary to visit any US territory we had to think of somewhere else. A pity as I would have liked to have visited these islands. However, it made no difference in the long run.

Antiqua to Saint Maarten

We left Antigua on 28 April, heading north to the strange island of Saint Maarten or Sint Martin, depending on whether you go French or Dutch! This island is split in two politically. Having sailed all night in good conditions we anchored in Simpson Bay, and eventually motored in to the customs dock, walked about 20 paces and checked in, and out, at the same time. After that we moved onto a berth in Simpson

Bay marina. Despite this being a European island, the power sockets were American, but with 230 volt, 50 Hz as well as the American 110 volt, 60 Hz. Both were available at the power pylons, but needed a different type of plug to any on board. I have no idea how the different cycles were achieved, never having encountered that before. An American plug is one I never expected to need so we all headed off to the nearby hardware shop. US$300 later I had a plug for the shore power lead. Talk about a captive market!.

After a slow afternoon checking out the bar and the local facilities, we retired for a good night's sleep on board with the air conditioner running.

Next morning, I rented a car, even though they all drive on the wrong side. We went off to see the world famous airport where you can stand on the beach, or hang on to the airport perimeter fence, and get blasted by the jet airliners taking off. If you turn your back to the runway you can watch the planes fly in over your head at very low speed and height on their way in to land. We had a good time on this island of two halves. There are no barriers between the different "countries" but there are noticeable differences in quality. I'd prefer to live on the Dutch side.

St Maarten airport arrival - 30 April 2017

Saint Maarten to Tortuga

7.30 pm the next night we left the marina and anchored off, ready to leave at our leisure. I checked all the steering connections, oil levels, etc and off we went.

It was another overnight sail to Tortola or Tortuga, depending on which name you prefer, a peaceful 85 mile sail. On arrival we spent some time motoring around to find the customs building. In the end we found the non-descript building on an ordinary concrete quay surrounded by truck tyres. I motored in ready to tie up and was peremptorily waved away. Apparently, I had to anchor off and dinghy in. The dinghy ride was about 500 metres to the unfriendly concrete dock. Having scrambled ashore I was then informed that I should be on the other side of the dock, but that I could leave the dinghy where it was this time! With everything done, I got back into the dinghy to find that it had now jammed itself under the concrete deck and I couldn't push it back out. I started the engine and put it in astern to help. Of course, the boat then shot back out and I ended up in the water. This episode reminded me of a comedy show! After much struggling and some help, I got back in, got away and went back to the boat. Whilst I was showering on board Michael and Jamie spread out all the wet papers and passports in the sun to dry. All in all no harm done but a lesson learned.

After several radio calls, we managed to get a berth on the village quay marina. We then spent another couple of days here, looking around and stocking up. All very helpful and friendly people, no pirates spotted and unfortunately no treasure found.

Tortuga to Republic of Dominica

On the morning of 4 May we left, heading NW to the Republic of Dominica, not to be confused with Dominica further south. The island is called "Hispaniola" and is divided like Saint Maarten with the western side being Haiti.

This was a 300 mile voyage, sailing almost all the way. Our charts showed a well sheltered long channel leading to several towns on the NE coast of the island, up a long wide inlet. The chart also showed a marina, about 10 miles up from the sea. As is usual with sailing plans, this was not how it worked out. However, the sailing conditions were excellent with an easterly breeze blowing us along on a very broad reach. The navigation was easy till we came close to our destination. There were several islands and reefs in the way, but all went well and we missed them all, it being daylight.

As we pulled into the first harbour, Santa Barbara in Samana province, we were met by Chico who advised that the marina was around the next promontory and was very expensive. This may even have been true, I never found out. He guided us onto a mooring that had been checked earlier in the year and was in good order. Again I don't know how true that may have been but we had no problems with it, nor with the weather.

We remained here on the mooring for three days, having a great time and even getting Internet in the nearest cafe on shore. One of the days Chico brought us on a tour along the north coast. Only perhaps 50 miles to a beach side town where we had lunch at a roadside cafe. A real tourist strip with many restaurants to choose from, and a replica pirate ship moored off from the beach. We had a most enjoyable day too.

Chico had arranged for the customs and immigration official to come into her office on the Saturday morning specifically to clear us out, with no extra charge for this weekend service. I would happily return to this area for a longer time, and explore further afield. Everyone was very welcoming and friendly.

Market in Dominican Republic - 6 May 2017

Beach in Dominican Republic - 7 May 2017

However, we had other islands to see and things to do so we left after three days and headed on to Inagua Island, the southernmost of the Bahamas. This leg took us two full days of motor-sailing in slack winds. At one stage we could see a major thunderstorm building up over the land behind us, but we did not encounter bad weather occurred. We had no problems on this leg, although there was a reasonable amount of commercial traffic around, ships, a tug and its tow and a dredger too.

Republic of Dominica to Inaqua

There is only one settled area on Inagua, whose name means no water, and that is Matthew Town with its lovely little harbour. Despite this harbour being totally reconstructed while we were present, the water was crystal clear. Whilst we were waiting for another boat to leave before we could tie up, we admired a fishing boat wreck on shore and the two decrepit trawlers tied alongside. Eventually we tied up alongside another, more respectable trawler against the quay wall.

One of the locals, Kevin, met us, adopted us and then drove us about 5 miles to the customs and immigration office. Here we were checked into all the Bahamian islands for a year, at a cost of US$300! Then back to the harbour with a small detour and a visit to the ATM for US cash, after which we could pay Kevin.

As we arrived back, I noticed US customs were all over one of the very sad looking trawlers tied up to the quay close to us. They were unloading everything off it and there was an unbelievable collection of junk coming off and being piled on the quay wall, such items as old beds, prams, concrete blocks and even an old engine. I assumed it was not the boat's engine!.

We arranged with Kevin for him to collect us next day for a tour of the island. As I walked past the customs officers, there were maybe 10 of them, I asked what was happening. Apparently, the main drug route here runs from Haiti to Nassau by sea, with the boats returning empty. This one, and the one tied up behind it, were being searched, looking for $20 million plus in cash that was supposed to be on board. We all promptly volunteered to assist, but were turned down.

As arranged, we went off with Kevin the next morning. We saw all the sights; the mountain of salt which is the only product here and flamingos. This salt facility works by the sun evaporating the sea water in salt pans, controlled by sluice gates and the business can export up to 6,000 tons per day if needed. As we moved along, we began to see pink flamingos in the marshy areas.

Salt in Anagua Island - 10 May 2017

Apparently, there are about 1,500 people on the island and half a million of these flamingos too. We learned that as the flamingos age, the pink colour gets darker. Having seen all there was to see on the island we returned to base and refilled the fuel tanks from the jerrycans. Kevin then brought us to his brother's house where he refilled our cans from his brother's 45 gallon drums of diesel, me with my fingers crossed as to the quality of this fuel, however it turned out to be just fine. All in all, this was a fun visit, but not to be repeated.

We left this delightful harbour on the morning of 11 May, with the US Coast Guard still pulling junk off the trawler, we never did hear if they found the pot of gold!

There's US$20 million cash hiding - 10 May 2017

Inaqua to Santiago

My initial plan was to sail to Havana, the capital of Cuba, on the north central coast. However, on looking at the charts and guide book in more detail I decided to go to Santiago de Cuba instead. This city is on the south coast, next to the American controlled Guantanamo Bay, and is the second city of Cuba. The main reason behind this choice was simple. Cuba is over 700 miles long east to west with Jamaica sitting due south of it and approximately in the middle so going to Havana would involve a minimum of 800 miles extra travelling at sea. Anyway we prefered to go to somewhere less travelled.

We had to retrace our course back to the eastern end of Dominica and then turn SW so as to pass through the Windward Channel between Cuba and Dominica with the normally favourable breeze, but we were motor-sailing again anyway as the breeze was light to useless.

It was good to see Cuba passing to starboard the next day and it wasn't long before the US military made radio contact instructing us to turn due south and remain 3 miles south of the Guantanamo Bay area. I asked if we could cut through instead as the sea was cutting up a bit rough, that was my excuse! After a few minutes the reply was no, and to reinforce this there was a big RIB next to us about 50 metres away with a large machine gun on the bow, unmanned but definitely available in a hurry. All we could see on shore were a couple of the big golf balls that radar installations hide in, otherwise it looked like any other bay. As we left the exclusion zone, we got a thank you and have a nice day on the radio.

It is a strange situation there as Cubans control the inner half of the Bay and the outer part is American.

Entrance fort to Santiago de Cuba - 12 May 2017

It wasn't long after that incident that we started to sail through a trail of plastic, especially polystyrene cups. As we tracked up this rubbish we came to Santiago where it was all coming from. We turned into the well-marked entrance under the imposing Spanish fort guarding the entrance channel. There were lots of small boats fishing inside in the enclosed bay, all enthusiastically dipping their lines. We kept going to starboard and then tied up as instructed on the radio to the quay wall. We passed by some badly damaged floating pontoons on the way, which we were told later were the remains of the Marina Marlin shown on my chart. A hurricane had passed by.

We were not allowed to set foot on land until all the clearance formalities had been completed. The marina people came over and helped with the lines, and plugged in the shore power lead, as the rules meant we could not even step onto the quay to tie up. They spoke some English and explained the check in procedures.

Next was an examination by a doctor. She took our temperatures and made sure we were healthy, then customs and immigration did their paperwork too. All very friendly and welcoming, and cheap. I'm not sure that many foreign boats arrive here.

We were hooked up the power, 240 volts, and then walked up to the office to sign up for our stay and arranged to remain for a week at the dock. There were some other foreign boats there, either at anchor in the bay, or tied alongside as well some having been there for months.

In the office I was quietly advised not to use the government owned hotels, restaurants, etc but to look for the private ones operating on the black economy! Excellent advice it was too, as the black economy is thriving all over the island.

$US is welcomed everywhere on this island, the Cuban currency being almost no use for tourists. The exchange rate in banks is extortion on a grand scale.

We got to know one of the local families here, having several meals with them and bringing them presents as well as paying our way. The son was very helpful to us and his sister was friendly too. I asked, after hearing complaints about the cost of vegetables, why they didn't just grow their own. The response was that someone would report this to the government and then they would be taxed on the produce. It was also explained that all cattle belong to the government and that anyone who killed a cow, even by accident, would be jailed for a long period, probably longer than for murdering a human!

We all took the local bus into the city which is some distance from the port and bought some Internet time there as well as having coffee in an old but well-kept government hotel. We passed the cathedral in the main square, an absolutely gorgeous building on the outside, but closed unfortunately that day.

The cathedral in Santiago de Cuba - 13 May 2017

Another day we spent looking around Fidel Castro's grave in the public cemetery. A big block of concrete with Fidel on a plaque is the headstone. There were other heroes of the revolution buried there as well, also commemorated on a smaller tablet on a wall. We were told that Castro did not live there even though he had been born in the area, but that the revolution had begun in Santiago.

On the same visit we all toured the museum that is dedicated to recording the revolution, full of memorabilia such as the guns used and many photographs of the heroes of the revolution, well worth a visit.

Fidel Castro's headstone - 13 May 2017

Of course, there were the famous old American cars on the streets, and they were so well kept, but most cars are old east European ones, and the many motorbikes are dirty and smelly old 2 stroke machines.

We took a trip in one not so well kept 1950's Dodge wagon. No rear seats, just wooden benches to sit on, and a Chinese diesel engine under the bonnet. In this we travelled to the nearest mountains, but after about 60 miles a half shaft in the rear axle snapped. No problem, the local bus took us on board and towed the wagon to the next small town. We all ended up in a seaside restaurant having pushed the broken-down Dodge from the road. We ended up having great food and an even better time. The restaurant owner having lived and worked in Canada most many years spoke good English and was most welcoming.

The owner/driver of the car removed the broken parts, had them welded and put them back in the axle. It was then that I noticed the lack of rear suspension and brakes! I'm not too certain that there was much oil in the axle either.

After all this we decided that, as it was getting late, we would not complete our trip but return back to the boat. However, there were three more stops along the way to retighten everything as all the vibrations kept shaking the wheel nuts loose, and then we ran out of fuel! No worries the driver walked into a local farm and got more fuel in exchange for his T-shirt. No money was exchanged as is normal here.

Cuban tourist car - 13 May 2017

There do not appear to be any litter laws in Cuba, as far as any of us could tell. If you're finished with packaging or bottles, anything at all, it's just thrown wherever you happen to be. Cigarettes are about 20 cents for a pack of 30, so everyone smokes and consequently there are butts and packets abandoned everywhere. I got a lift in the sidecar of a motorbike, with the driver, pillion and myself having a beer as we travelled. When we had finished the driver just dropped the empties over the side onto the road!

On our last day in Santiago, we went to visit a local cigar factory, government run of course. The idea was that we bought cigars at the factory shop, and at the government prices. As I only wanted a few I did so. Jamie and Michael went to one of the worker's houses and bought a whole lot more at a much better price. The black economy again.

We came across an English couple whose boat had been wrecked by a combination of a nearby reef and the Cuban navy. All they could salvage was their dinghy and outboard, neither of which was permitted to remain in Cuba. Since they could not just give them away, and obviously could not bring them on their flight home, I agreed to take these to Jamaica and leave them there for sale in the yacht club, which I did. Again, I have no idea what happened after we left.

18 May we untied, having been checked out and leaving some gifts as well, and set off for Montego Bay, Jamaica, our next stopover.

Santiago to Jamaica

It was a day and a half trip to Jamaica, with rain, lightning and strong gusts along the way. Jamie unfortunately was seasick again and was greatly looking forward to another stopover. By mid-afternoon we were tied stern to in Montego Bay Yacht Club, with power and water, as well as fuel. This yacht club has a spacious and open clubhouse with Internet freely available inside and a nice breeze blowing through while we were there. Food and drinks were also available.

We stayed here for nearly a week, relaxing and enjoying all the facilities as well as checking the boat and engines. I rented a car for the weekend we were there and, on the Saturday, we drove along the north coast to look at the luxury resorts and do a little shopping. We stopped at the famous Rick's cafe and had a coffee.

On Sunday we drove down south to Kingston, the capital, on the only toll road on the island. It had the advantage of no pot holes, but did have the odd landslide along the way! Kingston I found unimpressive and industrial and it felt threatening as well. We took the scenic route back following the GPS direction through the mountains until we could go no further. The dirt track had deteriorated into a rocky path. We turned around with help from some bikies who were going past and made our way back to a small town, with the fuel gauge showing zero fuel! and then back to the boat. Luckily the rental company didn't check underneath the car!

Having filled up with water, fuel and food we left Jamaica on the 25 May after an enjoyable visit. This time I was heading due south to Santa Marta in Columbia. Alas Jamie's seasickness returned with a vengeance in the rough conditions and, so to make life a bit smoother, we turned toward northern Panama instead. By good luck I had a brochure from an international marina company on board and found an IGY marina in northern Panama so that's where we headed.

Jamaica to Bastimentos Island

It was rough and rolly most of the way there, but at least we sailed on a broad reach which steadies the boat considerably compared to motoring but Jamie still had a lousy trip. Winds were generally easterly giving us a very broad reach, but quite strong, being force 6-7 all the way.

It took us four days to get to Bastimentos Island, and then to Red Frog Beach Marina. Despite the channel in being shown as clearly buoyed on my charts, there were no buoys visible anywhere. We later found out that when the commercial shipping channel was changed, travelling through a different entrance, all the navigation marks were removed and used in the new channel, very disconcerting. On our arrival at the marina, we were tied up to the main walkway near the entrance gate, with power and water, and the marina lent us a small ladder for convenience in getting on and off the boat. This was a lovely modern marina, due to be expanded not long after we left.

The marina manager, an American called BJ, looked after us extremely well, even paying the entrance fees himself to the Customs until I could repay him. Currency in Panama is the $US.

We had a superb time here, wandering over to a beach bar and cafe about 10 minutes away most days for lunch and a very cold beer, very welcome in the heat and humidity. There was a free water taxi to the main town twice a day, with banks and ATMs available. So we went across a few times to look around and restock our food stores. This was a really peaceful and relaxing time away from the crowds.

Refreshment in Red Frog beach - 1 June 2017

Bastimentos Island to Shelter Bay and Panama

I had been in touch with my agent in Panama since arriving regarding the timing of our canal transit. Boats doing this generally stay at Shelter Bay Marina at the northern end of the canal whilst the paperwork and boat measuring are being done. So we departed Bocas del Toro as arranged for the overnight journey to Shelter Bay Marina, and were accompanied by lightning storms all the way, fortunately inland from us. It remained dry the whole way which was good with 6 knots of breeze on the nose, not so good for us. It took 22 hours of motoring to get into Shelter Bay Marina. The lightning was a spectacular sight as it was virtually continuous through the night.

As soon as I informed the agent that we were in and tied up, he sent two of his people to the boat from Panama City, about 3 hours away. They brought with them a mobile phone, with credit on it and an invoice! They also took away the boat papers so as to get our transit organised.

We settled into the marina, checked over the boat, serviced all that needed servicing and went exploring both by foot and by taxi. However, Colon does not have a lot to offer and is not a secure town for visitors. It was so well named!

The Canal company's measurer was supposed to turn up the next day, but didn't. Then on the following day it poured with rain all day, and then on the third day, he eventually rolled up, unannounced.

We measured the boat's length overall. The measurer had arrived with his tape measure and whilst I held one end at the bow, including the anchor, he read off the overall length at the stern. Ships papers were not accepted for this. If the boat is under 50 feet length overall, including any overhangs, then the transit fee is about half what it would be for anything bigger, but you only get an advisor and not a pilot.

The marina was well equipped with power and water, as well as Internet and showers, etc. and is in very good condition. Very little seemed to have changed in the 10 years since my last visit. The aircon on board was very welcome again.

Panama and to Dublin

At midday on the 19 June, as instructed, we left the marina, avoided the shipwreck on the way out into the bay, and motored across the wide entrance to anchor in the waiting area, called "The Flats". Here we waited for our advisor.

We were too small for a pilot so we got a sort of junior version, a trainee pilot. This also meant we got a much cheaper rate for the transit, but no priority so small boats might have to wait many days for their transit to happen.

We were lucky with our timing due to spending our wait time in Bocas. At 7.00 pm that evening, with our advisor and four deckhands on board (Jamie, Michael and two Kiwis I had borrowed from other boats waiting on the marina), along with four long and heavy ropes I had rented from the agent that were required by the canal company, we headed to the first lock, having initially tied alongside a catamaran, with another, smaller, monohull on the other side.

There were no problems ascending through the first three locks, it's just tedious for small boats, even if you have a ship or two for company! That night we tied up to a ship's mooring buoy in Gatun Lake for a sleep. Small boats are not permitted to transit after dark under any circumstances, just too dangerous. The advisor was collected by a large steel launch, very skilfully driven fortunately as it could cause a lot of damage to a fibre glass boat.

Entrance to Panama Canal - 19 June 2017

By 7.15 am the next morning, with our advisor having made the leap from the pilot boat onto ours, we were off. This time I had Michael steer the whole way through Lake Gatun and the Gaillard Cut and then I took over in the Miraflores locks, losing my good floppy Sandringham hat in the process! These locks dropped us down on the Pacific side. Somehow this transit seemed faster and easier than the Atlantic one. We had a large ship for company behind us, but that was no problem as he waited until we were moving. The first time of transiting this amazing feat of engineering is fascinating, the second time you know what's happening and it's not very different to other, smaller canal locks.

By 4.15 pm we had returned the advisor and the ropes, offloaded the two Kiwis we had borrowed in Shelter Bay Marina, and tied up in La Playita Marina for the duration. I was going to Dublin, and Michael and Jamie were heading home having spent the best part of six months and 7,000 miles with me. They both said they enjoyed the voyage; I do hope so.

We spent some time exploring the area, including a nice restaurant next door and a burger joint further on. There was also a useful Yanmar dealer about a kilometre away.

We secured *BlueFlyer* well and arranged for the marina office to keep an eye on her in my absence, using the agent as a contact in case of any problems. I then got a lift to the airport with the agent. After a good flight I arrived in Dublin, checked into my hotel, having rented a car, and in the middle of the night got a phone call from Michael to tell me *BlueFlyer* was aground in the marina! It turns out that there was a spring tide that day. I arranged for Michael and Jamie to talk to the office and then move the boat to a deeper berth next day, before they flew home to South Africa.

~~~~~~~~~~

I had a successful trip to Dublin, meeting up with family and many friends in my hotel, celebrating Val's life and then scattering her ashes on her favourite spot where we used to go walking with the dogs.

Afterwards we all adjourned to the hotel to have an excellent dinner followed by a slightly liquid evening. In the morning all the family and friends started departing and before long it was just me, Fiona and her family.
~~~~~~~~~~

Chapter 9 - Panama to Tahiti

10 July - 30 September 2017
Chris, Gabrielle and Graham on board

Panama to Puerto Baqurizo Marengo

This was the longest part of the whole journey, about 4,500 miles with only two stopovers along the way, in The Galapagos archipelago and the Marquesa Islands. A long way for the new crew coming from Sandringham Yacht Club.

Chris and Graham arrived one evening having flown in from Melbourne. Their taxi dropped them at the marina entrance where I was waiting. After moving all of their luggage on board down the steep walkway – the tide was out - they soon settled in on board and had a good night's sleep.

Next day we went ashore to have a look around the local area. I arranged with the agent, I still had his phone on board with some credits available, to go provisioning in the commercial cash and carry shop in the outskirts of the city. He sent one of his employees with a pick-up truck to bring us around the various shops etc as we required. The cash and carry wholesale shop was a Costco-sized area in Panama City and before we left it we had filled up four trolleys and then loaded the contents into the pick-up truck with the driver helping.

On the way back to the boat we had a couple of diversions. I called into the local chart shop and got some updated Admiralty charts for the Pacific. From there we went to the nearest fuel station with all the empty jerrycans and filled them too, much easier when the transport was available, but we still had to bring them down the marina to *BlueFlyer.* Unfortunately the marina did not have any trolleys or wheelbarrows so after several trips up and down the marina, eventually we got everything on board and stowed away.

Shopping Mall in Panama City - July 2017

We all decided to dine out at the local bar and restaurant about a half kilometre walk that evening. The food and service here was good and we had an enjoyable evening.

Whilst returning from the restaurant I managed to break my foot splint while walking down some steps, the broken part gouging my shin. This foot support had been an expensive carbon fibre job from the USA. Although I don't use it on the boat, and it wouldn't be needed till we got to land again, this was not a welcome development with the islands that were ahead. I emailed some pictures to the seller in Melbourne and was asked to bring it back to them. After I explained to them where I was and what my plans were, we agreed that I would give them the bits on my return in about four months time. I'm sure that my reason for this delay caused some chat at tea time!

Monday 10 July saw us leaving La Playita Marina, having filled the main fuel tank on the way out, and heading out into the approach channel, heading south west for all of 30 miles to the Las Perlas Islands in the Gulf of Panama. The channel was extraordinarily busy with large shipping going into and away from the Canal and we had to fight our way between them. I'm sure this little boat was a thorough nuisance to all concerned.

Although the Las Perlas islands are Colombian, they are holiday spots for Panamanians too, but we didn't have to check in or out. In the end we only stayed one night and didn't get ashore as the rain was miserable and the seas somewhat rolly. We anchored just off Contradora Island at one of the hotels for the night and left the following morning, heading out into the Pacific Ocean to the Galapagos, about 1,000 miles west.

All that day we had ships, dolphins and rain for company with almost no wind so we were, again, motor-sailing. For the next three days we continued to travel under main and engine, with clear skies and starry nights, interspersed with squalls and lightning. This wasn't a bad start for the new crew to get to know the boat and we were making progress.

On the night of 16 July, we were hit by stronger winds and heavy waves in a lumpy sea. The night was pitch black with nothing visible, even the moon was blacked out by the clouds. These conditions lasted throughout the night and were not at all comfortable.

During the morning we had an overflight by a helicopter, in the middle of nowhere. He circled us once or twice and then flew away to the west, perhaps Galapagos. I am still puzzled by this, who it was and what anybody could be doing this far out.

My daily inspection of the boat revealed a nasty problem developing. The port side lower shroud had started to unravel during the rough weather. This is the support for the middle of the mast and is made up of 19 strands of stainless wire twisted together with a crimped clamp at each end and it was the lower end that had broken on a couple of these strands.

Temporary rig repair - 17 July 2017

Chris and Graham managed to rig up a reinforcing rope from the sliding ring attachment on the front of the mast which is normally used for the spinnaker pole, to the deck fitting. The ring, which can be pulled up and down a track on the front of the mast, is not meant for this but served us well.

Using a turnbuckle to help tighten this homemade mast support we carried on towards the Galapagos Islands as it was impractical to return to Panama as we would have been pounding into the wind and the seas, causing more damage and a lot of discomfort on board. We kept on going, hoping that the Galapagos would have the necessary repair facilities as it is the first stop along the Pacific to Australia.

Next I found the generator had been covered by sea water, presumably from water coming on board during the heavy squalls overnight and, although it ran, it was not producing any electricity! It had also turned rusty overnight.

During the night we had sighted, and passed by, St Paul's Rocks. These are deserted rocky outcrops and not normally on the route to Galapagos, but we had been pushed somewhat south by the conditions. That night they were very forbidding, being steep to and very wet, as well as being totally isolated, not even a light showing. This was not a spot we had intended visiting as there was nothing visible other than rock.

Gradually the sea and wind conditions improved to the extent that late in the evening on the 17th we hoisted both sails and turned off the motor. We could finally sail our course to Isla San Cristobal and our anchorage, still over 150 miles away. Our position at this stage was about 150 miles south of the equator and we were all having to wear sweaters and jackets at night! It was not particularly warm.

Finally, on the afternoon of 18 July we anchored in the busy bay/harbour of Puerto Baqurizo Marengo where we would be cleared into Ecuador, these islands being Ecuadorian. The harbour was full of visiting yachts and local tourist tour boats, some of them were big and modern cruising ships. We found a spot to anchor not too far from the shore with good holding in the sand.

Having contacted the agent on shore he came out to us with a bunch of officials and his bill! On payment of some of the bill, we didn't have enough cash for all of it, besides it was a bit cheeky of him to expect full payment before doing anything, he got the customs and then immigration to clear us. This was followed by a diver hopping over and checking the hull for cleanliness, despite showing the certificate from Panama.

The diver cleared us and then it was fumigation time, again despite the Panama certificate for the same procedure, the wrong chemical having been used. The official doing the fumigation had a problem as we did not have any 240 volts on board. We all went ashore and left the fumigator to it. On our return later we found a certificate on the table showing the boat had been debugged successfully, I doubt very much that he had done anything other than collect a fee.

I explained the rig and generator problems to the agent, no problem was the reply, I know just the people. He later returned with a "rigger" who looked at the damage, measured lots of things and then said he could do nothing to help, and presented his bill for immediate payment.

On the generator front, an electrical engineer from the Coast Guard was promised that evening. He did turn up and had a long examination of the generator, and then explained he needed to get a capacitor.

After all that checking, we all had coffee on shore in a café soon to become our favourite because the Internet was available, slow and expensive, but beggars can't be choosers. The coffee was good though.

We stayed on this island for two enjoyable days, exploring the area on foot. The turtle research station and a couple of volcanoes were examined.

I found and checked out a local hardware shop hidden away on one of the backstreets. I found some stainless turnbuckles and stainless wire! Chris and Graham went back the next day and bought them. We then used these to reinforce our repairs to the rigging, using a very strong dyneema rope around the mast spreaders this time tied to the new turnbuckle so as to be independent of the existing repair. To really be sure we used the stainless wire as well on another turnbuckle, also as an independent repair.

Temporary rigging repairs - 29 July 2017

Chris discovered that a nearby boat was owned by an American sailmaker and his wife who were heading to New Zealand to start a new life there. As we had some damage to the genoa, we dropped it, bagged it and left it on his boat for repairs. It came back a day later fully repaired at a reasonable cost and we hoisted it back up the forestay.

The electrician returned as well and managed to get power from the generator, I'm not sure how though, as no capacitor ever showed up. I reckoned we would have to try again in the Marquesas for both repairs.

Finally, we left the anchorage early one morning and set off to Isla Santa Fe and the anchorage at Puerto Ayora, otherwise called Academy Bay. All these islands had English names, but they were changed to Spanish ones when Ecuador took over ownership. It took all of 4 hours to sail to the new anchorage where we dropped two anchors, one out the bow and the other one at the stern. This stopover gets very busy so the authorities insist that no boats are allowed to swing around their anchors, thus the two anchors. This means a lot more boats can be packed in during the high season.

We went ashore, by water taxi as dinghies are not permitted. They will probably be damaged by the taxi operators if left unattended. This means more employment for the locals of course. The town had been transformed since my last visit, there were paved roads replacing the cobbled ones with small traffic jams. Also new were a hospital and supermarkets. A far cry from having to get ashore before dawn and get to the local markets before everything was sold out, not that there was ever very much to start with.

We filled up the fuel tanks from the jerrycans and then I brought the empty ones to the only filling station in the islands for fuel, as I had done on my previous stopover, so that we were full of diesel again. There did not appear to be a fuel barge in the harbour anymore, no loss as boats got free water in their fuel when refuelling from it.

Chris and Graham went off exploring again and we arranged to meet up later for a meal somewhere in the town. I noticed that all the seals that had lived on any unwary boats, afloat or ashore, had vanished during the redevelopment works, however there were still one or two at the fish landing area, along with pelicans, all looking for free handouts which they got too.

The restaurant we chose was on a side street near the end of town. The entire street was closed off and all the restaurants put their tables and chairs out on the roadway for the patrons, thus increasing the number of diners considerably.

Next up for us was the trip to the Marquesa Islands, about 3,000 miles away. I expected a slow trip of about 3½ weeks duration based on my previous journey, somewhat slower due to looking after the rig damage. This problem was causing me a lot of concern. On reflection I think the temporary repairs were a lot stronger than the original!

We left at 11.00 am in the morning, there didn't seem to be any reason to rush off, and headed to the south of the next island and ended up having to squeeze upwind to pass the Tortuga Rocks. This was done whilst motor-sailing as we were in the wind shadow of the islands. Whilst we were doing this the depth gauge kept showing that we were in very shallow water, although all the charts showed we had plenty of depth. I now think that we were passing over a thermocline, or warm upwelling current giving false readings.

Later on we stopped the engine and went sailing as the wind had picked up, so all was quiet on board, what a relief. We were doing about 4.5-5 knots on a course just south of west and pretty much on the rhumb line to Hiva Oa. This was about 30 miles north of my course of 10 years before. I noticed that we had a nice current with us of about 2 knots, in other words, 50 miles a day free! We didn't have this free travel previously.

The wind speed stayed in the 10 to 15 knot range and south easterly and our speed over the ground gradually rose to around 7 knots with the help of the current. Speed over ground is what it sounds like as opposed to speed through the water.

The weather remained mainly good but would occasionally become overcast. We decided to reef down the mainsail so as to improve the airflow to the genoa and so keep the speed up and also to stop the sail collapsing and then opening again with a bang. Not good for the boat or the crew, especially with the rigging problem.

Several fish were caught along the way, and eaten with gusto, mainly Mahi Mahi which are a beautiful fish to both look at and to eat. The conditions really didn't change much for several days. We experimented with poling out the genoa, and then tried to goose wing it - have the sails out on both sides. Simultaneously.

At one stage we were cruising along at 8.5 knots, peaking at over 10, whilst taking it easy on the rigging! Most of the nights were clear and bright with so many stars on show that they were uncountable, and the moon was shining brightly as well. All very ideal night time conditions.

We sailed on and on the deep blue sea, still heading the right way. I would check the course by the sun twice most days. So long as it rose behind us and set ahead of us we were going the correct direction! We got to the halfway mark soon enough and well ahead of my time scale too.

During the next half of the trip, we saw a ship! It was visible for a few hours and made a very welcome distraction and talking point.

The winds were gradually forcing us south of Hiva Oa so we decided to go to Fatu Hiva instead. This is not a check in place but we thought we'd call in for a night anyway as there's a reasonable anchorage at the Bay of Virgins and a very small village too. This was now only 900 miles away, almost in sight!

At one stage I slowed us down to around 2 knots and filled one of our water tanks with the desalinator as we had emptied them all, not a problem as we still had plenty of bottled water to drink. After filling the tanks we continued on engine only as the wind was hopelessly light, and this would give the batteries a good charge too.

On the second last day we got some breeze again and so put out the headsail to increase our boat speed.

On the last day, with Fatu Hiva in sight, we passed by Motu Nao. This is the tip of a seamount and is barely 2 metres out of the water, very dangerous at night, but clearly marked on the charts. It's much too low to have a navigation light on it. That evening we entered the Bay of Virgins and dropped the anchor far up inside the well sheltered bay. We had made the Marquesa Islands safely and four days faster than the previous trip too. 2,600 miles at approximately 140 miles a day.

We lifted the dinghy off the foredeck and dropped it into the water and then headed into the tiny little harbour there. We tied off the dinghy to some of the seawall rocks and clambered ashore.

The only notable thing about this island was a small waterfall about a 30 minute walk away, otherwise it was a scruffy little volcanic island with a few hundred people scratching a living. There was no shop or fuel station and if we wanted to buy anything it was by barter for alcohol of any description. Alcohol is a major problem in this island chain, and we had been advised not to give any to the locals.

We didn't buy anything needless to say and departed the next morning for Hiva Oa, arriving early afternoon in Atuona, Baie Tahanki. These islands are all volcanic, very imposing high peaks and usually with several bays in which to anchor and go ashore. They are also well covered with very lush tropical vegetation.

We all checked in at the Gendarmerie. Because I had an Irish passport, I was exempt from needing a bond or a return flight so no problem. The others with their Australian ones, had return flight tickets from Tahiti. If you don't have these then non-Europeans have to pay a returnable bond. I suppose it keeps illegal immigration under control. This check in was not the full procedure, no customs or health checks, so we would have to do it all again in Tahiti on our arrival, but it was great to be there.

Our anchorage was somewhat rolly, even with a stern anchor holding us into the swell, but all the boats here had the same problem. The dinghy was much used to get ashore every day and sometimes twice a day. Just at the inner corner of the bay was a service station with a small shop selling basics like bread and beer, fresh baguettes every morning, as well as fuel. It's the only fuel station on the island.

Again, I tried to have the rigging seen to. There is a boatyard here and the owner/operator came out to look but could do nothing to help. Another "electrician" checked the generator and ordered a new capacitor from Tahiti at great cost. When this was fitted, having been flown in, it made no difference, there was still no power out. This problem had been happening intermittently since the whole thing got wet and rusty.

As well as these problems a loud groaning noise had developed in the steering. This was quite worrying as it could mean several rather serious problems such as the rudder about to fall out! I snuggled down in the stern locker and checked everything that I could and then gave all the turning pulleys and other moving parts a big spray of WD40. Later Chris also did the same though neither of us found any problems. On checking the rudder later back home no problem was found.

We refilled the fuel from the service station, and enjoyed some Internet in the town, as well as exploring the area. The Paul Gaugin Museum was examined, the bank was successfully checked for cash and the Post Office promised to deliver various cards to Australia.

We stayed here for four days of relaxing time, although it appeared that the island was swaying a bit every time when we went ashore! The landing platform wasn't great, being somewhat rickety and broken with many ropes tying other boats to the shore.

Eventually we set off to Tahuata Island and anchored in Baie Hanamoenoa in company with some other boats. I had been here before and knew that once the anchor was set it would hold well in sand. This was a much bigger island with roads and traffic as well. I noticed a new landing quay on the north side, with a fuel depot. There were some strong wind gusts while we were here, but no problems.

I did some small maintenance jobs on board, and a bit of cleaning. It was here that Gabrielle joined us for the trip to Tahiti. She flew in from Melbourne to join Chris on board.

We stayed here for a couple of days and then went over to Baie Vaitahu. After an overnight here, during which Chris went for an involuntary swim from the dinghy, we moved back to Baie Hanamoenoa as it was too rough to get to Hiva Oa that day. Next day we motored on to Atuona Bay in Hiva Oa with no problems, although the current in the channel between the two islands can be up to 8 knots so tides are important here!

On 29 August we weighed anchor in Atuona and left in the late afternoon for Nuka Hiva, about 90 miles away. This is the big island and is the capital of the Marquesas. We arrived in Taiohae Bay at 9.00 am after a smooth sail and found a spot to anchor reasonably close to the shore. There were many boats here and the landing stage was crowded with dinghies, but no problem to climb up a ladder and get ashore.

Unfortunately, this island has a contaminated water supply due to the multitude of goats and other wild life that live up in the catchment area, so we could not fill the tanks from shore. When I asked why there was no filtration, I was informed that the French government had built one several years previously but that it no longer worked! I suppose the natives are immune to whatever might be in the water and anyway no one appears interested in fixing it. We got to know a lovely couple here also travelling on their boat, he was Australian and she was American.

After a few days we set off again on 2 September heading to the Tuomotu Islands. These used to be called the Dangerous Islands, being really low coral atolls on the route to Tahiti. The highest point on all of them being the tallest palm tree. For all of that these are the most beautiful islands with great diving and snorkelling in crystal clear waters.

Initially all we had was rain and squalls, with little wind, so we motored out for some hours before putting out the reefed main and the full genoa, heading south of west with an ESE breeze. The steering noise was gone, and so was the port navigation light! You may win some but the Gods always want their reward.

We were sailing on a regular sea, with good sunshine and an almost full moon at night, so easy watches with "Otto" doing all the hard work. What a great crewman "Otto" was. No food, no water, steered a constant course and never argued! All he needed was a few volts.

On the 5th we put a big reef in the main to slow down so that we would arrive in Rangiroa in daylight, with the sun overhead. This meant that we could see through the water with polarised sun glasses and spot any obstacles, such as coral bommies in the way. It's generally better to miss them!

By 9.00 am on the 6th we could see Rangiroa ahead and I headed into the southern pass and on to anchor off the Kia Ora Hotel in the clearest water you can imagine. We met another boat, bigger than us, coming out as we entered and he was being tossed all over the place, quite a spectacular sight as it was a lot bigger than *BlueFlyer*. The entrance and the channel are well marked by navigation lights, with a wrecked boat on each side to keep the helmsman concentrated on his job.

At anchor in Rangiroa - 7 September 2017

As we had been checked in at Hiva Oa and Gabrielle on her arrival at the airport, there were no problems in heading ashore. The Kia Ora Hotel is definitely upmarket and very comfortable. The extremely helpful reception arranges tours, etc for guests but would also do so for us.

We found a sort of supermarket with everything we would need just up the road from the new to me harbour. The harbour had a good landing area, as well as a ferry quay and several tour boats. Nearly everything has to come by supply ship from Papeete, which in turn gets deliveries from New Zealand by ship and by air from France. You can imagine the cost of goods.

Chris and Gabrielle took a room in the hotel for a couple of nights whilst Graham went walking to explore and I went looking to see if I could rent a generator. There were none available on the island so I could not use the desalinator to fill the water tanks. We just drank the bottled stuff from Nuka Hiva.

On the 11th we moved over to Avatoru village which is on the NE pass, about an hour away. We anchored off here in a strong tidal flow. I had visions of losing the anchor when we left due to being unable to lift it from the rocky bottom. As the dinghy was in the water there was a visit ashore, and then lunch. Back on board we looked at the perfect conditions for going through the pass, pulled up the dinghy and then the anchor, fortunately with no problems, and set off for Tahiti, only a couple of hundred miles away.

We didn't have enough wind to stop the engine until early evening, but at least the batteries were fully charged again. On checking the rigging the cap shrouds and the lowers were noticeably slack on the leeward side. This meant that the windward ones were stretching, not good, but I knew that there were several riggers in Papeete.

The sailing conditions were lovely, not quite enough wind so slow going at 4-5 knots, but not a problem.

On approaching Papeete, we dropped the sails and started the engine. For once we had a problem in that it began cutting out, sounded like fuel starvation. I pulled off the pipe work between the tank and the engine, but no blockage there. I then poked a wire through the pipe that comes out of the tank and felt a blockage which cleared. The engine then ran well again for a short time before slowing down and then stopping. I switched the fuel feed to the forward tank and all was OK again. Another job waiting for me.

When you enter Papeete it is compulsory to contact Port Control for clearance. This is not for keeping clear of any shipping, it is so that the Port Control can contact the Air Traffic Control to get permission for the boat to pass by the end of the runway. You really don't want a 747 or other aircraft hitting your mast!

Having got the required permission, we then entered the harbour through the pass in the reef and tied up to the visitor's pontoon on the

City Marina. This was a new marina, only three years old. I went to the marina office and checked in, and was given a berth nearby. I also bought an electricity and water card as both of these are metered and expensive.

Having secured the boat, we all went ashore into Papeete city. It's a very busy bustling town, noisy and a bit smelly after all the clean islands we had visited on the way. However, it had a plethora of cafes and restaurants, all with bars attached, so we felt right at home!

Next day Chris and Gabrielle took themselves off to a hotel, from where they would depart to Melbourne, via Auckland.

They returned to help Graham and I remove and bag the genoa for repairs. I had contacted a sailmaker, a rigger and a general mechanic and arranged for them all to come down to the boat, as well as my agent ashore who I had used previously on the WARC.

Mat, the rigger, came first and took all the measurements needed to replace all the rigging. Luc then arrived and we decided to polish the diesel in the fuel tank, which was almost full of course. The sailmaker took away the genoa.

As well as all this the agent came over and we contacted a friend of his who also had a boat in the harbour. He came on board the boat and I arranged for him to mind *BlueFlyer* in my absence. I would be going home for six months so as to avoid the cyclone season, and see the family again.

Luc and I took a long look at the generator which by now was only producing smoke! SOPOM, the generator people on the island, gave me an enormous quote to replace it but Luc and I decided we could do it at a much better cost. I would get a replacement one delivered from the UK. The original generator had come from Queensland but the dealer there wasn't interested in supplying another one, unlike the UK.

Luc then polished all the fuel, finding that it was spotless. Another problem to solve! I found the problem eventually by removing the primary fuel filter and examining its parts closely. Eventually I found a small O ring with a small split in it allowing air into the fuel line. Unfortunately, engines don't run on air!

~~~~~~~~~~

I arranged for all the repair and replacement work to be done on my return, as this suited all of the contractors. Graham soon departed for home and I moved the boat to a different pontoon as requested by the office as the boat would be deserted for six months and the berth I was on was one that they used for short term visitors.
~~~~~~~~~~

The day before I was due to fly I took off the Bimini and the spray hood as well as the boom tent and stored them below. The outboard I put into a lazarette and I moved the life raft to the front of the cockpit table. I put a fortune into the electricity meter, tidied up as much as possible, had a final night on board and then flew home for Christmas.

Docked in Papeete - 17 September 2017

Chapter 10 - Tahiti to Fiji

24 April - 22 June 2018
Garry, Dawn and Meg on board

Tahiti to Bora Bora

It was now March 2018 and I had returned back on board *BlueFlyer* again. It was a long, but very enjoyable six months break in Melbourne, during which time we, the family, decided to knock down the house and build a new one.

As it turned out there were no cyclones that year in the Tahiti region, and just as well too seeing as how the marina suffered badly in just a harbour swell!

During my long return flight from Auckland, I crossed the Date Line again, and that meant I arrived the day before I set off! All very confusing. However, it did make up for my becoming a day older when I flew the other way.

My neighbour on the flight from Auckland, after some chatting, turned out to be the Minister for Revenue and Ports in the Cook Islands. An interesting man to talk to and we would meet him later on in the Cook Islands. I thought him quite young for such an important position in a government but have since learned that not only has Mark been re-elected but has also been promoted to Vice Premier. Mind you most people still working look young to me!

We discussed all sorts of subjects during that flight, especially how to promote the islands and increase the number of private yachts visiting the islands as most visiting yachts spend money locally on repairs, restaurants, etc. He gave me his card and asked me to call him whenever we arrived in Rarotonga.

I had a severe panic moment when I thought that I'd left the boat keys behind at home, but I found them OK in the bottom of my carry-on bag. No need to turn the flight around!

On arrival I picked up my baggage, having passed through the welcoming committee of singers and musicians, no lei of flowers this time, too late I supposed, and then found a taxi to take me to the B&B I had booked for the night. This was a private house just outside Papeete in a quiet street and I had a peaceful night followed by a delicious French breakfast in the morning, and then got a lift to the marina in the owner's car. She had no idea where the entrance was and dropped me quite far up the road, for a fee of course!

I had received a message from Mike, who was minding the boat in my absence, to say that the marina leg *BlueFlyer* was on had broken up in a heavy swell, but that I was not to worry about it as there was no damage to the boat and that he had moved her back onto the arrivals pontoon with the help of the marina staff. Not great news when you're several thousand miles away!

After I had arrived back to the marina, I looked at the broken pontoon and thought that *BlueFlyer* must have been holding it all together, since there was only a strip of aluminium about 100mm long holding the remaining parts together. I also found out that this was the second time that this pontoon had been destroyed in the three years that this marina has existed. Mike informed me that he had put out extra fenders from his own boat for added protection and that the engine start battery had been totally flat despite being on charge, so that meant buying a new one.

Once on board I spoke with Mat the rigger regarding the timing of my rigging repairs having met him whilst I was walking to *BlueFlyer*. He asked that the boat be moved onto the other big marina here, called Taina marina. I had been moored on this one previously and it is far better sheltered, being about 7 miles away from any waves or swell that might come through the entrance pass and was well inside the barrier reef. Beside all that it has a proper quay wall as a barrier. There are several other advantages here as well. For a start the power and water charges are included in the berthing fees, so no stupid card system and no running out of power. Another is that there are two restaurants, a bar and a chandlery owned by an English speaker within a couple of minutes' walk and there is free WIFI at the office, whilst it's open.

There is a big Carrefour supermarket in a shopping mall, and a smaller one at the local service station, both within walking distance and both of them have no problem with people bringing their trolleys to the marina, in fact they have a weekly trolley collection service that returns them. As well as all that I was moored within 30 paces of the fuel depot where you get the duty-free stuff.

The two marinas cost much the same in high season, but the City one is half the price in low time which is why I had left *BlueFlyer* there for the time I was away, having checked with my insurers that this arrangement was acceptable to them.

Whilst I was in Melbourne I had arranged for a new generator to be delivered to Papeete. This one came from the UK agents, Advance Yacht Systems, the Queensland agent apparently having no interest in supplying another! His loss was my gain as the price was cheaper and the warranty considerably better too. It arrived as promised and was cleared fairly quickly too with the help of Bernard, my agent. Luc, who had looked at the fuel on my arrival, picked it up in his van.

With the help of Mike and Bernard I shifted the boat from City Marina on Sunday but had to tie up overnight to the entrance wall as my berth was not yet decided, so I didn't move onto the proper mooring until early on Monday morning.

Next morning after I had the boat tied up on her correct mooring Mat appeared, checked all was good to proceed and then parked his van on the quayside behind *BlueFlyer*. He and his assistant seemed to have a complete rigging workshop including generator and hydraulic press in the van as well as the necessary coils of wire for my boat. Mat was hoisted up in a Bosuns Chair many times during the week and I know his young assistant was very grateful for my electric halyard winch. It was amazing to watch Mat remove the rigging wires one at a time and fit the replacements as he made them up in the van. I could see why he wanted the boat in this marina, it was so much calmer than the City Marina.

His procedure was to take down one old wire, bring it to his van on the seawall, make up the new one and then get hoisted back up the mast to fit it. He did this with all nine of them over three days. Of course, they were all fairly slack when fitted and, once all the new ones were in position, he took hold of the lower spreaders and violently shook the mast to make sure the foot was fitting into its shoe properly. His last two days were spent tuning the rig and replacing some halyards that were getting on in years and usage and then also end for ending the main sheet, as well as fitting two new jib sheets. There were no problems encountered.

When Mat had finished and been paid the balance of his account with a small bit of help from my insurers, I got Luc down to the boat. We moved *BlueFlyer* to the outside of the marina wall temporarily so that she could lie alongside and thereby be much closer to where Luc had his van.

I had already removed all the generator fittings previously in preparation, and so we lifted the old set onto the cabin floor using the new main halyard and then checked the new generator's dimensions, they were identical. We hoisted the old one out with the main halyard and winch and then I cleaned out the whole area, which really wasn't all that dirty, just dust.

Once I was ready, we reversed the process and lowered the new genset onto the existing base. The hardest part of the job being persuading the very stiff and short exhaust hose to go into the soundproof box and then onto engine! With that done we moved *BlueFlyer* back into her marina berth again. The following day Luc and I finished the job and commissioned the generator, no problems at all. I had taken the precaution of photographing all the electrical connections on the old set. So we knew exactly where each belonged.

Luc also brought down the new engine start battery which we fitted and connected, but only after making up new terminals. The old bits and pieces were taken away by Luc even though I was supposed to take the old generator out of French Polynesia in order not to pay duty and taxes on the new unit. Luc was thinking of fitting a different alternator to the engine and that is why he was happy to take it. The old battery went for recycling.

The next week was spent cleaning down below and scrubbing the dust, footprints and bird droppings off the decks. I could only do a couple of hours of this early in the day due the strong sun and humidity. I spent some time with soapy fresh water trying to get the clear panels on the spray hood clean, but really they had been disappointing and had not coped at all well, having become cloudy and difficult to see through.

We had found that two seacocks had ceased working properly on the last leg and so I had them replaced by a local. He free dived with a hammer and plugs and fitted the soft wood plugs to the through hulls prior to climbing back onto the boat and removing the faulty cocks. He took these away to buy replacements in Papeete. Unfortunately, it turned out that no direct replacements were available so in the end he bought several parts and adapted them to fit, so all was well eventually, and we didn't sink. I found this lack of fittings a surprising problem as the boat was built in France.

This same guy found two new stainless hinges for me to replace the one that had broken on the top step of the companionway. I fitted both the new ones in place, although they were not quite the same as the old ones.

Next up was getting the outboard checked. It had refused to start and was putting petrol in the water as well when I tried to start it. This was taken away by the diver/seacock fitter and a couple of days later it came back, running.

Following the recommendation of the agent I got an electrician down to check the forward navigation lights, if you remember one failed. He spent several hours in the sail locker checking and replacing as much of the corroded wiring as possible and got everything working again. I also asked him to look at the radar which had stopped working somewhere along the way, perhaps while the boat was left for the six month break. His report, with photos, was depressing, as the business end up on the mast had corroded badly and could not be repaired. A new one could not be sourced on the island so that was a job for later, in Australia probably.

16 April and Meg was arriving, with Dawn and Garry the next day, so it was just as well I had all the laundry done by the agent, Laurent, and the empty gas bottle refilled. At that stage I seemed to have run out of repairs, although the hull was booked to be cleaned the next day by divers, there being no means of hoisting the boat out of the water. This was successfully done as arranged. All the new crew arrived successfully and were soon on board making themselves at home. Dawn and Garry were of course familiar with the boat.

20 April we all took a four wheel drive across the island almost to Little Tahiti, the appendage that hangs onto the SE end of Tahiti by a narrow strip of land. The central area of Tahiti is very high and rugged with dirt roads or tracks with the occasional concrete bits. At one stage we crossed a bridge that was only half there, and still being worked on. There was plenty of wild life as well as beautiful flora to admire. However, there was no way an ordinary car could travel in these areas and survive.

We also looked around Papeete and did various bits of shopping, both for souvenirs and food.

Garry and I managed to get all the jerrycans filled early at the duty free, having got the required paperwork from Laurent a little early. Then he and the others went to Papeete to pick up some tax-free drinks.

At this time the government elections were being held on all the French Polynesian islands and as a result on the day of the voting all the bars and off licenses were closed to prevent anyone getting drunk and causing trouble, as if that would work! However, restaurants serving food could also serve alcohol, this meant we had to have a meal with our beers, G&Ts, etc, a real hardship, but we all struggled through.

Looking down on Papeete - 20 April 2018

Mid-morning of the 24th saw us leaving Taina Marina and heading off on our next leg. Admittedly only to the neighbouring island of Moorea, all of 6 miles away. It was so nice to sail again with a sound rig and a clean hull. The refreshing sea breeze on our faces was lovely too.

Just as we were leaving I received an email from my son-in-law with an attatchment. On opening it I found a bill from Telstra for $25,000! Thinking this was a joke by Noel I didn't take too much notice. However it turned out to be genuine. I emailed Noel and asked him to see what he could do as I could not deal with it. Telstra was not the least bit helpful and refused to investigate. Eventually I got it sorted on my return to Melbourne several months later, and managed to get my cancelled phone number reinstated as well. No one could tell me how this bill had occurred and I could only hope it would not recur.

We anchored that night in Cook Bay, along with a few other boats. Although it was raining heavily, we still managed to dinghy ashore for a tasty dinner in the local restaurant that was almost falling into the water, it was overhanging so much. We watched the fish swimming around underneath whenever the owner threw some waste into the water. That night there were several strong wind bullets off the surrounding hills but we never shifted.

We only stayed one night here and moved on into the next bay, Opononhu Bay. Not long after we had arrived and anchored the *Paul Gaugin* cruise ship dropped by for a few hours and very quickly had their lifeboats ferrying passengers to and fro to sightsee on shore.

We remained here for another three days, relaxing and sightseeing, nothing too strenuous, but managing to eat and drink well. We did however move anchorage to further out from the shore the day after arrival, as a precaution in case strong winds might move *BlueFlyer* ashore.

Saturday the 28th and we were off again, heading to Raietea, sailing with reefed main and a full headsail. This was an overnight sail, but we didn't get there! We ended up in Huahine instead, not a problem, just that the course there gave us a more favourable wind direction. The moon was full and bright that night for our sail and we were in company with a couple of other yachts which is always good. Everywhere we went we would come across a boat or two from the latest WARC rally so it was usually a race to see who could get a mooring or a good anchorage before everything was snapped up.

We spent the day at Huahine on anchor, had a great lunch at the local cafe, and then in the late afternoon moved to another anchorage, just because we could! After a peaceful night we set off for Fare, a town up the east coast, only a couple of hours away. Here the local shopping centre was not very far up the road from us, it was busy but we picked up a few things all the same.

Monday 1 May, saw us depart Fare and head over to Utaroa on the northern coast of Raietea, having got a favourable breeze. The mooring that we picked up there belonged to "Dream Yacht Charters" and cost us a slab of beer for the night! Once secured we all went ashore to pay our fee and look around.

We bought dinner that evening from a 'roulotte vendre' ashore, these are the mobile food vans that are common on all the islands. The steak, chips and salad meal was delicious. After an excellent night on the mooring, we moved on to a quayside in the harbour. There was another yacht (German) tied there as well and the crew came over to enjoy a beer or two and a chat on board with us.

Next morning we had breakfast ashore in a patisserie, a busy place but with excellent food and service, after which we set off for Tagalog, under engine in the slight wind. We anchored in Haemene Bay, where Meg, Dawn and Garry all had a tour of the local vanilla plantation, and brought back some pods which went into two duty free vodka bottles on board. After lunch I raised the anchor and we headed to Apu Bay. I picked up a free mooring there for the night. We all found it hot during the day, probably not helped by being in this very pretty but enclosed bay.

Our final trip in these Friendly Islands was to Bora Bora and the yacht club there. I was trying to get to the club in time to grab a mooring before the WARC boats took them all as this was their rendezvous spot prior to their clearance and departure from French Polynesia. The anchorage here is very deep and, having dragged my anchor on a previous visit, I knew that being on a mooring would be so much easier and safer all round.

I succeeded too! We had a great time here for four days, enjoying the shore facilities in the "yacht club", including Internet bought by the hour. Good food and alcohol at a reasonable cost, for Tahiti that is. The yacht club is no more than a restaurant and bar with minimal facilities for visiting yachts. I thought that the island was even more tourist oriented than before and, to me anyway, has become a tourist trap. Whilst we were on the mooring, Garry and I spent a little time under *BlueFlyer.* With the help of diving gear we replaced the anode on the propeller shaft.

Bora Bora to Rarotonga

Anyway, on 7 May, we motored around the nearby headland to the fuel dock to top off our fuel and water, and then on into the harbour where I went to the gendarmerie to get final clearance from French Polynesia. This was not as easy and as quick as I had planned. It turned out that there was a wrong date on one of the papers and that took several hours, and many phone calls, to sort out. At one stage we were going to have to stay for two more days due to it being "Le Weekend" followed by a holiday. However, all was well and in the end we set sail for Rarotonga, the capital island of the Cook Island archipelago, in the afternoon. Dinner that night was curried chicken under full main and reefed genoa. Night watches were started, 3 hours each throughout the nights from now on.

That night we were blessed with heavy rain squalls and lightning too, followed by calm conditions, but we were still making good speed towards our destination. The next day had occasional wind gusts to around 30 knots but nothing too serious.

The night of the 8th was another story altogether. We had winds to almost 50 knots with variable directions, accompanied by appalling rain showers too. We all got soaked despite wearing our sailing jackets. We all survived the stormy night but in the morning, we found the support for the boom, called a vang or kicker, had been damaged overnight and was lying on the deck instead of being attached to the mast foot. This would have to be repaired or replaced in Rarotonga as a matter of necessity. I also found that the boom had been resting on the spray hood and had worn through some of the fabric, another repair!

Anyway, we carried on sailing and sometimes motoring as well in much better conditions, and eventually we saw lights ahead of us, approximately 10 miles off. The sea was still lumpy and unpleasant after the storm. As it was still dark, we slowed up to arrive in daylight. None of us knew what to expect in the harbour as none of us had been here before. There was no reply to any of my radio calls to shore which I found a bit disconcerting. We later found out that no one does anything till at least 9.30 am.

In the heavily overcast daylight, we motored on into Avatui harbour and secured ourselves to the quay wall, behind a commercial ship but outside the security gates. We all then tidied up the boat, had breakfast and waited and waited for the various officials to appear. Obviously there was no rush as it took a couple of hours for quarantine to turn up, on his own. He cleared us and said customs would be along. Another wait and no visitors. At this stage I think we were all having doubts about staying here on Rarotonga, especially as the only way ashore that we could see was by clambering up and over a filthy black truck tyre.

I then rang my new best friend, at least on Rarotonga, Mark Brown, the government minister from the flight to Tahiti. He actually remembered me and said we could go ashore, saying that Customs were under his department, but he would come down anyway. We all climbed ashore to stretch out a bit. Mark arrived soon afterwards, gave us a cheery welcome and said that we should all go to the local market just over the road, after all, he said, he was the boss of the customs.

This market was held every Saturday and was quite obviously much better organised than any of the others we had come across to date in the Pacific. It seemed strange to me to hear nothing but English being spoken, especially in a Kiwi accent, and having the area clean, no litter. I bought a local SIM card for my phone and checked out emails, etc, as well as enjoyed a fresh hot coffee whilst strolling around.

Eventually the customs did arrive, fortunately after we had returned to the boat, and cleared us in, swearing vengeance on Mark for his action in releasing us when they learned that we had all been ashore already.

At the same time the assistant harbour master asked us to move away from the quay wall, which was for commercial ships use only, and to moor Mediterranean style against the adjoining quay wall, using our anchor as the bow retainer and tying the stern off close to the wall. None of us were too happy with this arrangement as the wall was covered in old truck tyres, OK for ships, but not small boats like us. We ended up lying with the bow pointing straight at the harbour entrance. This arrangement also meant we had to use the dinghy to go ashore at a ladder further away. We had to stay about a metre off the tyres so as to avoid hitting them in the swell.

The swell was gradually growing and this meant adjusting the anchor tension frequently to hold us in position away from the wall, an altogether very unsatisfactory arrangement, and we still touched off the tyres anyway.

Garry and I took the broken vang pieces off the boom and over to a local machine shop as suggested by the Harbour Master, who also gave us a lift there and back. He was also kind enough to transport us to a second-hand marine store cum breakers yard to see if we could find a suitable replacement for the vang. No luck there so I asked the machine shop to make up a new rigid vang from some suitable alloy tubing that was on the rack. I had a long look at the pieces and thought that I had never seen such thin tubing doing such an important job on the boat. I chose the tubing this time to make up the new unit.

The guys in the shop did the work quickly and efficiently and the new vang was ready a day later.

Garry and I brought it back to the boat and fitted it to the boom, a perfect fit first time, and the correct angle on the boom too. This is vital to have correct in order for the mainsail to roll away properly. I could have adjusted the fitting on the boom if needed but I really didn't want to.

I also looked at the stern light which had stopped working on the way over, nothing complex, just a corroded connection. A bit of cleaning, some gaffer tape and all was well.

We rented a car for the couple of days on the island and had a look around. This isn't a big island but it does have some real beauty spots around the coast, including an extraordinarily beautiful lagoon, very well sheltered, but unfortunately too shallow for boats to use.

We all went to a dinner with a show on one of the nights, a spectacular rendition of an old tale of inter-island war and peace with a beautiful girl involved! A well worn story.

Whilst she was there Meg bought a very nice ukulele, for use in Australia only by her son. Although she was concerned that Australian Customs might confiscate it being made of wood, we all assured her that this would not happen, and it didn't.

By now the swell inside the harbour was becoming increasingly worrisome and bigger, and because we were not at all happy with the anchor's holding power on the unknown harbour bottom, we decided to fill our fuel tanks and head off. This was earlier than planned, but necessary for our safety in this harbour, and was partially brought on due to a night spent adjusting the shore lines to keep us away from the quay wall.

I had been in touch with another of the Cook Islands, Palmerston Island, earlier, who in turn put me in contact with a family on Rarotonga, with a view to carrying anything needed, or a passenger, to this isolated island.

The family came down to see us not long after our arrival and asked us to carry a couple of boxes for them. This we were very happy to do, and just before our departure they returned with two or three cardboard boxes for us.

Prior to our departure I had to go to the offices in town to get our clearance to leave and our passports checked and stamped as usual. You aren't allowed into the next country without the clearance paperwork from the country you're leaving. Then the Customs arrived at the harbour and photographed our leaving in somewhat cold and wet weather. I think both of the officials remained in their car.

Rarotonga to Palmerston Island

We left the harbour on 16 May, heading north west to Palmerston Island in a rough sea, the wind having gone more northerly. This is one of the smallest and most remote islands in the Cooks group. I had obtained the special permits needed to visit there from customs and immigration before leaving Rarotonga. Normally there are about 63 people living on the island, but it turned out that one person had gone to New Zealand for medical treatment and so the entire family went too, all paid for by the New Zealand government. That meant there were only about 30 members of the families left on the island.

This island is unique in that there are only three families resident here, all descendants of one man from the UK who obtained the island back in the 18th century from the UK government.

He lived there until his death with his Polynesian wife and her two female cousins. Thus the three branches of the same family.

It took us a couple of days to reach the island, mainly motor-sailing through some squalls and heavy rain showers, along with the mainly light easterly breezes with occasional stronger gusts. On arrival, having made contact by VHF radio, we were met by Edward Marsters, the customs official and policeman, followed by his cousin the immigration officer, and mayor of the island. We took a mooring as requested and also dropped our anchor as recommended, just to be sure. We were on the leeward side of the atoll and so had comfortable sea conditions.

Moored and anchored off Palmerston Island - 19 May 2018

As soon as we were ready and had the paperwork done on board, we were taken ashore by Edward and his son John to a warm welcome. The route through the surrounding reef is impossible to follow unless you live there and use it frequently, so we were very happy to be transferred by Edward. It's mainly unmarked, but there was the occasional stick jammed into the reef for guidance and, I suspect, for the well being of visitors.

When you arrive here you are met and adopted by one family and looked after by them, in this case it was Edward's. We met the family and had a delicious lunch in the house with his sister and mother, and delivered the boxes, before going for a stroll around the island. This is a typical sandy coral island. Actually, there are several islands within the reef but only Home Island, or Palmerston as it's called, is occupied.

There was a solar power farm and a building full of batteries being charged by the solar, also a diesel backup generator. There is WIFI here but the Internet is very slow through a satellite link, so after we tried to contact the outside world a few times we gave up. No harm.

The only real trade on this island is frozen parrotfish that breed and grow extremely well in the lagoon, and these are fished in a very ecological way. There are several very large commercial freezers, usually full of the fish awaiting transport, all powered from the solar rays. They are in Bill Marsters house, which was combined with a bar and yacht club whose walls are covered by burgees and photographs left by visitors, a museum of previous visitors and the island's administration office, Bill running them all! He also has the ice cream store for the island in another freezer.

The island has a church, which had been moved in the past due to waves washing around and undermining its original position, a community hall, several houses, a health clinic with a nurse and a main street of brushed sand. The sandy side paths are lit by solar lighting \.

We were shown several heavy construction machines on the island that had been presented by Japan and China to help with various big projects but have since been pretty much abandoned due to the costs involved in removing them from the island. This is the same fate that is in store for the two large aluminium landing craft type barges and their big outboards, specially constructed for the purpose of getting the big machines ashore.

There are one or two wrecks that have been salvaged from the reef whose parts may be used at some time in the future, who knows, including one large marine diesel from an American yacht. Absolutely nothing is thrown away here. Water is in tanks filled by the rain and there was no fuel available.

It appeared that nearly everyone living here was on a pension of some sort from New Zealand, nobody had a business type job as such as there was simply no need. This life is perhaps the nearest to idyllic that I've come across. No requirement to work and more money than needed to live off. However, the policeman, Edward, as well as the mayor, Bill, received salaries for their hard work as well as their pensions.

We were invited to attend the Pentacostal Sunday service in the church, with the normal acapella singing, followed by a feast nearby, full of delicious food.

Before we left I gave a lot of spare rope, an angle grinder and a spare hand held VHF radio with charger and spare battery to Edward to add to his stores, there being no payment required for the mooring or the hospitality. What an amazing stopover this was.

We left this idyllic spot on 21 May, now heading west to Niue, another bigger independent and isolated island. We were again battling with the WARC boats to get a mooring there. Although it was only 300 miles to Niue it took us three days to get there in very light winds, so motor-sailing or just motoring the whole time.

Such breeze as there was easterly so right behind us, the most inefficient point of sailing for us. This was a quiet leg with mainly clear skies and plenty of stars at night. Eventually we sighted the very flat island of Niue in the distance, there are no hills, and made our way to the anchorage where we got one of the very few free moorings left.

Niue is an independent island, but closely linked to New Zealand economically and socially, as are most of the islands in this area. It also has some of the best looking currency around! Anyone for a triangular $2 coin?

Having tidied up the boat and put the dinghy in the water we then faced the next challenge - getting ashore! The landing here made St Helena's one look like a walk in the park. I'm sure on a day with no swell this is an easy operation, but we didn't have any such day during our stopover.

The sequence is that you first come into the jetty in your dinghy, remember there was a minimum swell of at least half a metre, and grab a rope that hangs down from a crane above on the quay. Then you move the boat into the steps. These steps are about 80 cm high and are constantly being drowned by the swell. Once there everyone, bar one person, clambers gracefully ashore, whilst getting well wetted below the knees. The remaining person on board then has to hook the crane to the dinghy bridle. He then clambers ashore, same wetting process as everyone else.

When all this is done you then hoist the dinghy up with the electric winch, store it on dry land and Bob's your Uncle. What could be easier? What could possibly go wrong? Returning is pretty much the reverse operation, and equally wetting!

On our first visit ashore, we contacted customs who told us to wait at a small covered sitting area just up from the harbour. When asked for how long we were told maybe a couple of hours! On hearing that we walked up onto the roadway above, passing the unfortunately closed yacht club, and by following our noses found a cafe. Coffees all round and some slow Internet there too. This cafe was frequented by us and some of the WARC, as was the Indian takeaway next door.

Eventually we returned to our holding point and then the customs, etc arrived in a rusty people carrier and cleared us in without any bother. Their delay had been caused by the daily incoming flight landing and having to deal with the passengers, then followed by the outgoing people flying away. They gave me a lift up to the cafe where we had got our coffees earlier.

Now that we were legitimate again, we returned to the cafe for lunch and drinks. We were chatting to the WARC officers there who told us there was a storm predicted to be coming this way early the next week. This was not good news at all as there's no proper protection anywhere from the waves and the surging swell that arrives ahead of any storm.

We rented a car and had a look around the island over the next couple of days. We arranged this through the tourist centre cum art gallery a few paces further up the road from the cafe. There's really only one road on the island. It had been built by the Americans during World War II and goes right around the island, possibly a 3 hour trip if you stretch it. We did stretch it and on the way we saw lots of abandoned properties and not much sign of prosperity at all.

Next day we found the international airport and a supermarket style shop. On Saturday we returned to the shop and restocked the boat food, carrying all our purchases back on board via the landing steps. We also ordered several takeaway meals from the excellent Indian restaurant as meals on board.

We drove up the low hill above the town for a look around, finding the hospital and lots of Pacific Ocean to see, but no sign of any storm. However all the locals were confirming its arrival with the heavy swell to appear first so we decided to head off the next day. We returned to the airport for immigration clearance and then found the customs offices buried in a small industrial estate and cleared out with them too.

We returned the hire car by leaving it at the tourist office with the key in it. No crime here, it's just too small an island.

Niue to Tonga

8:00 am the next morning, 27 May, we let go of the mooring and set off again, the course being just north of west heading to the Kingdom of Tonga, about 280 miles away. Our destination was Vava'u and the port town of Neifu.

On this two-day leg we managed to shut off the engine for most of the first day, the rest was motor-sailing again! The wind backed around from SE to SW through north and all points in between. However, we kept going at around 5 knots, most of the time in the light winds and flat seas.

We heard later that the promised storm and heavy swell never materialised at Niue. This caused considerable loss of income to the locals.

The beautiful entrance to the harbour was through wooded hills and past small wooded islands into the harbour of Neifu. The actual port area was a not so picturesque town and wharf. We secured ourselves to the fishermen's wharf just in front of what looked like an abandoned fishing trawler, and waited for the clearance officials to deal with other boats that had arrived before us.

When all the paperwork for clearing in had been completed we motored over to the mooring field, found a suitable mooring spot just behind a floating wreck and tied-up to the buoy, glad to be here and intrigued as to what was ashore.

All into the dinghy and ashore, landing at a cafe bar right on the seafront, with WIFI, food and drink, overlooking the moorings. We stayed there for some hours and had dinner there that night, not a bad meal, and all speaking English too.

Next day as we walked around the town, I discovered that my Australian bank card would not work in either the ATMs or the banks and so had to use my Irish one instead. This kept happening all the way back to Australia. My Australian bank said there was no reason for this from their end, there must be bad contact at the island ends. A pain but not important as it happened.

We spent a lot of time in The Tropicana bar whose owner, a Kiwi, was helpful, especially with getting all of our paperwork ready for Fiji and Australia, all for a fee of course! I later found out that he was the Ocean Cruising Club Port Officer.

Garry rented a maxi taxi for a couple of days. It had a considerable amount of duct tape holding it together, but it worked OK. We used it to bring the new vang to a boatyard machine shop where we arranged to have the lower end reinforced and the swivel plate on the mast replaced, both had bent on the trip from Rarotonga to here.

On the way back to the boat we called into the local motor parts shop to buy some more oil and filters. It turned out that the owner had met Garry at some conference previously. No discount though! Whilst we had the car we did some diving in the stunningly clear warm water.

All in all we spent a week here, exploring by the rent a wreck and by *BlueFlyer*, including a visit to the Botanical gardens, unfortunately closed that day. This Tongan Island is beautiful but it's not the main one, that's further south and has both the king and the government on it.

We happily motored *BlueFlyer* around to a beach resort not too far away and anchored off. We dinghied ashore for drinks and ended up having dinner with the manager and his wife, both Kiwis. A very pleasant evening was had followed by a good night's sleep.

Next morning we sailed over to Horseshoe Bay and then to Maurell Bay, spending peaceful nights at both. There were so many sheltered bays to anchor at here, each different to the other and all very secure from weather problems.

Meg tried painting on the beach but was totally defeated by the mosquitoes, which was a shame. Eventually we returned to Neiafu and a different mooring.

I had our empty gas bottle refilled and arranged to fill our fuel tanks and jerrycans the next day prior to departure. I also arranged to anchor off the boatyard to pick up the vang, and pay for it too. I did all the paperwork as well in a cafe the owner of which helps everyone, for a fee.

As arranged, we returned to the fishermen's wharf for the diesel as well as for health and customs clearance. The fuel tanker was already there filling two other boats before us, but as soon as he had done them, he drove away!

We phoned the fuel arranger and asked what was going on. He rang back to say that the tanker had run out of diesel and would return in a couple of hours. The health inspector had not turned up either so Dawn and Garry chased up customs to see if they knew what was going on. Customs eventually got hold of the doctor in the hospital. Apparently, she knew nothing of our departure and promised to be down as soon as possible. Island time is wonderful!

The tanker did return eventually, but then it turned out that he only had a big nozzle on the fuelling hose that would not fit into the neck of the jerrycans, but did fit the deck filler. Out with the funnel, followed by very slow filling but eventually the job got done, and the lovely lady doctor turned up too. She stamped some paperwork without looking at any of us on the quayside and then drove away again, cash in hand.

We motored off when all the fuelling and paperwork was completed, back to the same anchorage at our favourite beach resort for dinner that night. Next morning, we motored around to the boatyard and our vang.

Garry went ashore and returned with the fitter plus the vang. This was then trial fitted, removed and brought ashore for modifications. This happened twice more before everyone was happy. I paid the bill. Finally we were on our way.

Crew on a beach in Tonga - early June 2018

Tonga to Fiji

Next stop was Port Denerau in Fiji, 550 miles further west towards Australia. It was 6 June when we left Tonga with sails and engine pushing us along at about 5 knots in flat seas and a not great NE to SE breeze again. We did manage a full days sailing about halfway across but this constant motoring was very disappointing to us all, not at all what we had anticipated in the Trade Winds belt, but distinctly better than the alternative of no wind at all.

On the 10th we crossed the 180 degree meridian and so our positions changed from east of the line to west, a great point on the journey. Next one like that would be the International Date Line.

That day passed with the same conditions and so on we travelled until we sighted Viti Levu on the horizon, Fiji at last. We carried on to the south of Suva, the capital, until we came around the western end and on to the entrance pass.

This gap in the reef is about 300 metres wide and well marked as the commercial shipping use this channel too. It wouldn't do for an oil tanker or cruise liner to pile up on the reef. There was still several hours motoring to reach Port Denerau from the entrance. We did try sailing again but soon gave up as you do need some wind to sail and so carried on just motoring along.

I had contacted the main marina for a berth, but there was only a mooring available, about 100 metres off from the main shopping and restaurant strip on the seafront.

After we had tied up to the mooring, we waited a while for all of the officials to come aboard. They turned up in a big new looking rib and climbed aboard. A rather large young lady had to have some assistance to accomplish this manoeuvre!

All was in order and all our papers were suitably banged on and stamped. We then had to run them all back ashore in our little dinghy, another interesting manoeuvre! I don't think they were too impressed with our small dinghy and outboard, but they were successfully landed.

So for us it was all ashore for coffees and buns of some sort, and then on to the marina office. I booked us on the mooring for the next three nights, and also arranged a lift out and cleaning of the hull. I called into the marine services building next door and arranged for new anodes to be fitted to the boat and for a service to the outboard.

Before the lift out took place, we went exploring Port Denerau on foot. Again my bank card would not play ball at the ATM but there was no problem with the Irish one.

This was a pleasant town, even if it is entirely for tourists and is full of restaurants and boutiques, etc, as well as a lot of tour boats, dive shops, etc.

We found the Port Denerau Yacht Club and called in for drinks. This is just another bar and restaurant, nothing to do with yachts.

We again rented a car for a few days and drove around, found the Nadi airport, more or less by mistake and had a look around Nadi, not much to recommend it, but we did come across a Chinese owned supermarket on the road back. No idea why it was out there all on its own. We took advantage and did some shopping. A very well stocked supermarket and friendly staff too.

As *BlueFlyer* was going to be on the hard for a night we booked a hotel, the Tania. This one was about a half hour out of town, very comfortable, with excellent food and drinks, as well as air conditioning and TV in the rooms, and showers that didn't move with no limit on the water supplies.

On the 13th we motored around to the travel hoist where Avi, who worked for the marina, lifted our home out of the water and onto the hard standing. Once he had really carefully chocked her up, he set to with the pressure washer. The hull was not all that dirty and quickly cleaned up but there was a colony of mussels on the top of the rudder. That took Avi a while to clean.

Once Avi had finished Baobab Engineering took over. They cleaned the propeller and shaft, which were very dirty and then recoated them with 'PellerMax' anti foul. As this had to dry overnight, we were booked for an extra night at the hotel. They also replaced all the anodes and cleaned and anti-fouled the bow thruster. The new propeller that had been fitted before I left Sandringham had disappeared, and this made the thruster even weaker than it was normally.

I checked the rudder for play, after the noise heard earlier in the voyage and found that there was almost none, and what there was due to the leverage from a 1.8 metre long rudder. On checking the keel and rudder I found no damage; this was fortunate considering we had bumped into something earlier in the voyage.

The outboard was fully serviced. It had apparently been under water; I can only think that happened at Christmas Island during the heavy rain.

On the hard in Fiji - 13 June 2018

Next day we were back in the water and *BlueFlyer* took off like a young kid again, with the clean hull and clean propeller.

To celebrate we sailed over to the Musket Cove Marina and Resort for three nights. We motored through the reef around Malalo Lolai island into the bay, and then through the anchored boats before carefully heading in through a very narrow cut and onto the marina. We moored stern to the walkway, using the bow anchor again. Shore power was promptly connected so that we had air con and full batteries again. There were only a few boats in here so the bar on a sand island that was about 20 metres away didn't get too crowded, a very well arranged setup.

I checked in at the office eventually when someone turned up! Then it was a short walk to the main resort building, complete with restaurant and bar. Last time I was here we had stayed in one of the Bures, or bungalows, that are here for guests. This resort is a very cool and relaxing place with all the amenities a holiday maker needs, including Internet. We all managed to enjoy the break here, especially with the local bar being so near to the boat!

On leaving we hauled our anchor, and another boat's as well. No problem to sort out as the dinghy was still in the water and Garry quickly untangled us.

We sailed off stopping and anchoring at other small islands as we came across them. Some were uninhabited and some with families living on them. These idyllic islands were in the Yassawa group. I had visited some of these before on a friend's boat. We had lots of swimming and snorkelling but no diving as it was mostly too shallow. The waters were crystal clear and with plenty of fish, and other wild life to look at.

One of the days was spent anchored off the Manta Ray Resort where we had lunch and snorkelled on the beautiful coral gardens in front of this resort. There was quite a current running here with the tide in the channel, so you entered the water at one end of the beach and ended up at the other.

Another night was spent on anchor between Navarro and Vanuatu Levu islands. We had a beach bonfire with the crew from another boat also anchored there for the night.

Finally, on the 20th we returned to a different mooring at Port Denerau. Next morning I snagged a berth for us whilst another local boat went off for a week of cruising. We shifted ourselves to this berth for a couple of nights whilst we stocked up on food, water and alcohol, before filling up with diesel on the fuel dock.

Departure for Noumea in New Caledonia was on 22 June at 10.00 am, so a leisurely start.

Chapter 11 - Fiji to Sydney

22 June - 19 July 2018
Garry, Dawn and Meg on board

Fiji to Noumea

I had picked up several weather forecasts, including one from my weather router in Perth, all showing good trade wind conditions, so we had no qualms about departing Fiji and heading to New Caledonia.

Having motored through the same reef pass that we had come in through, the breeze being on the nose, we found the seas outside were lumpy and the wind SSE to SE, just where it was supposed to be. We had company through the pass of a large dredger type ship, heading to Suva, AIS (Automatic Identification System) gives out a lot of information.

That day and the next were spent sailing along in warm conditions with light cloud and 15-20 knots winds, giving us 6-8 knots of boat speed in the right direction.

We had to do some motor-sailing the third day due to light and variable breezes. This continued on and off until we reached Noumea. Not unpleasant conditions, although we got some cold southerlies for a time with confused seas and not quite so pleasant conditions, but that was for a few hours only. Mostly we had light fluffy clouds, big moons and a multitude of stars at night.

On the morning of 25 June we sighted some islands to the north of us. Initially I thought they were dark clouds on the horizon but they remained visible for a long time without appearing to move. In the end we concluded, correctly, that they were the Loyalty Islands lying along the east side of New Caledonia. I didn't think they would be visible from our position.

It was another days motor-sailing till we reached the SE entrance channel leading to Noumea at around midday. Nearly there we thought, but no, there was still another nearly 40 miles to reach the town.

Strong outgoing currents delayed our progress through the pass as we passed several islands, with the famous Isle de Pins visible. Eventually however we reached Noumea and found at least six marinas, few of which have names on them. I spent a fruitless hour trying to find our marina berth in entirely the wrong marina! Eventually our prebooked marina gave us the latitude and longitude of their entrance. We were only about 5 miles away! Very fortunately the girl in the office spoke excellent English. Then we motored up to the correct marina with the name displayed and tied up on a visitors berth as instructed.

We walked up to the office where I was given a form to fill out, this was immigration. We were then instructed to wait for a couple of hours on board for customs to arrive. If, after that time they hadn't appeared, we would be free to go ashore. They never appeared. Apparently this is normal. I signed up with the marina for the two days booked and was told that staying any longer was on a day-to-day basis only, depending on demand.

Next day I took a taxi to immigration and got stamped in properly and then the following day the bio inspector came and took our rubbish away. Amazingly, all formalities were free of any cost, the one and only time this ever happened.

The marina was happy to have us stay tied up for as long as possible, after all the berth was not free. The instructions were that if we hadn't been asked to vacate by midday then we were OK for that night. Mind you the marina was full, but in the end, we stayed for a total of 12 nights!

On going ashore legally the first stop was at the nearest bar restaurant, all of 50 metres from the office, more hardship! Coffee was good and, as we later found out, so were the beer and the food, this is France after all. Cheap and plentiful baguettes again, bliss! There's a lot of English spoken here in the port area, I suppose due to all the Australian boats and tourists that come. This is the finish point of several boat races and rallies every year.

We spent a very agreeable time here, walking around the harbour and into Noumea itself. We dined several times at the 'roulottes', cheap but good food. We enjoyed the baguettes for breakfast and whatever we fancied at night.

On one of the evenings, we met up with the local Ocean Cruising Club officer and went out to dinner in the local yacht club, a real one this time.

On another day we travelled up to one of the hills and admired both the superb views and the wartime cannon on the peak. This was one of many that protected the islands from invasion during World War II. It was installed by the American army.

The Pacific islands do like the Americans due partially because the US army built a lot of the existing infrastructure to protect them from invasion and then because they cleared off after the war. This is in stark contrast to the British and French colonists who seem to have looted the islands and then stayed on anyway.

Relict from World War II in New Caledonia - 1 July 2018

We liked the tall straight pine trees, similar to Norfolk pines, and the bright red soil everywhere, they reminded us of Australia. Meg took off for a couple of nights away on her own looking over the eastern side of the island, staying with local families, the rest of us stayed on board.

I did some engine servicing and general checking over on the boat, discovering that we had cockroaches living on board. As they were not paying any expenses and were making a mess, they were sprayed with

Mortein, which they didn't appreciate at all. Dawn bought some bait boxes and put them around too. In the end we eliminated them all but they had made a terrible mess of some spare linen in one of the lockers in my cabin. I ended up throwing some of it away.

As we had in Fiji, we enjoyed very much our stay here, but eventually had to leave, after all Garry had to return to work, the end of his long service leave was approaching rapidly. So having refilled everything that needed refilling we said our goodbyes to the other boats on the marina we had got to know and left on 8 July. I had informed the Australian Border Force that we were aiming to check in at Sydney in about a week's time, and then I filled out the long form received via Internet and sent it back.

Noumea to Coffs Harbour

Not everything goes to plan however. The first day was spent with the engine on in very light breezes, but heading on course. Over the next week's sailing we were slowly but surely pushed north of our route by the winds and ended up pointing to Coffs Harbour, well north of Sydney.

We had some cracking sailing and some very light conditions too. As we approached the coast, we ran into SW winds, neither favourable nor pleasant, and some really horrible choppy seas, so another alteration to our course as we diverted to Yamba - Iluka on the Clarence River, just to confirm our decision some really heavy and cold rain hit us on the way. There we anchored mid river with our yellow flag flying enjoying what turned into a lovely sunny evening on board. There are no check-in facilities here so no one was permitted to come on board and we were not allowed ashore. I checked in with the local Marine Rescue people who, I'm sure, kept a watch on us for the Customs in Coffs Harbour.

To celebrate our return to Australia we opened the bottle of French champagne from Noumea that Garry had procured and the tube of Pringles as well as other nibbles and demolished them all in the cockpit, enjoying both the warm afternoon sunshine and being safely back on home soil, well almost on shore.

We contacted Border Force in Coffs Harbour to tell them of our diversion. The officer said that we had been expected in Sydney and why had we diverted? I just said that weather conditions had made it imprudent to carry on to Sydney and that we should be in Coffs the following day, but late. The late bit was caused by a Sunday arrival and me being unwilling to pay the double overtime charges involved. We were instructed to anchor in the harbour and contact him on Monday morning after 10am.

Very early next morning we left the Clarence and headed south to Coffs Harbour under full sail. We passed by several whales on the way, all heading north, but none too close. This turned into a fine, warm and sunny day all the way, with good sailing conditions.

As we approached Coffs Harbour I slowed right down so as to be too late arriving and then rang the Border Force office to tell them that we were going to be too late for today but that we would anchor in the harbour for the night as requested. On entry I found one of the two moorings laid in the inner harbour was free so we grabbed it.

Next morning, I rang the office and was told to go into the marina berth and there would be an officer there waiting. We did this, but no officer there. After about 15 minutes he arrived, this one man turned out to be the Border Force in Coffs Harbour! Very friendly and efficient, he only took 15 minutes for inspection, health and immigration formalities to happen, and a $350 charge, that's why I wasn't happy to pay overtime as well.

After we had been cleared into Australia, I walked over to the marina office and met Elise, the manager, who I had met 10 years previously on my way south. She is also the Ocean Cruising Club officer here.

I arranged with her to stay a couple of nights on the marina, which wasn't too full, so no problem with space. Then we went off to walk around, finding the yacht club and having dinner there. All was good and we were enjoying the warm weather and being back in Australia again.

On the next day we were surprised to meet George and Robyn from Sandringham Yacht Club at the fuel dock. They were delivering a yacht up north to Airlie Beach for race week, motoring the whole way. As they couldn't stay it was a very brief meeting indeed.

On 17 July we moved over to the fuelling dock ourselves in between fishing boats and filled up again before heading on south to Sydney.

Coffs Harbour to Sydney

It took us two more days of sailing and motoring in quite variable breezes to reach Sydney. We had no strong winds but we did however have the East Australian Current with us, 1½ to 2 knots in our favour. We reached Sydney Heads late on the second night and then slowed down as we were in fact booked into Cronulla Marina, south of Sydney, and I had no wish to arrive in the dark.

There is a wide entrance to Cronulla but that is followed by an awkward and skinny channel right up against the shoreline, with a 90 degree turn into another equally skinny channel. It's easy to go wrong, but I had been there twice before, so knew what to expect.

We were expected and the staff there guided us onto the fuel dock which is right next to the marina office. This office is a converted flat-bottomed houseboat.

I checked in and, as we were already tied there, used the time to refuel before motoring out to our pen. Meg hopped off the boat, took a train to her house and then returned with her car about an hour or so later. We helped her load all her bits and pieces, including the ukulele, and the pod in vodka, and then she was away. Dawn and Garry headed off as well to stay with some friends locally, and I remained on board, suddenly on my own again.

On their return Dawn and Garry packed up most of their stuff too and headed off to the airport and then to Melbourne, I stayed behind for a day and then locked up *BlueFlyer* and went home too via the airport. In the end *BlueFlyer* was on her own for a month in this marina, being well looked after.

Chapter 12 - Sydney to Melbourne

21 - 26 August 2018
Eric and Amo on board

Via Jervis Bay, Eden, QCYC and SYC

Poor old *BlueFlyer* had been left all alone on Cronulla Marina whilst I was in Melbourne, but at least this time the marina remained in one piece and she was regularly checked by the marina staff.

The only reason for this long pause was the weather. I had to wait for a window of reasonably favourable conditions before heading off on the final leg, the prevailing winds being south westerly, in other words, right on the bow.

Finally, everything seemed good to go weather wise. Eric, Amo and myself would bring the faithful boat home at last.

The plan was for Eric and Amo to fly up and stay on the boat, with me following on Tigerair the following day. Alas the airline decided to cancel my flight whilst I was in the airport, with no availability till the next day!

Back to the airport the following day, to see my flight was on time. I went to check in and found the notice board was incorrect and the flight had been delayed for 2 hours.

I rang Eric to tell him as we arranged to meet at a local Chinese restaurant in Cronulla on my arrival. We had eaten there before so both Eric and I knew where it was.

It so happened that as I arrived at the marina in a taxi from the airport, the others, including Meg, were there with a takeaway box for me! I just had time to say hi to Meg before she drove away.

I enjoyed the curry for dinner that Eric had bought.

We spent a quiet night on board prior to the morning departure. The water and fuel tanks were full, and the other two had bought some food for the journey, so we were all set to go. There was still a good stock of canned food on board, along with long life milk, juices, and other food in the fridge and freezer so we weren't going to starve en route! In fact, we never seemed to have had that problem, this boat having been very well stocked throughout, thanks to all the different crews.

21 August and we were on our way south finally. Our first stop was at anchor in Jervis Bay at the Hole in the Wall again, having had strong winds and lumpy seas all day, with reefed sails, and the engine helping by times. It was good to be securely anchored that night in a secure and sheltered place.

Next day's plan was to sail overnight to Eden at the southern end of New South Wales which would involve an early start. Instead, we ended up waiting for the strong winds to abate, which they eventually did in the early afternoon. After an overnight trip we motored into Eden to find much better conditions than the last time we visited. We tied up alongside the same wharf as before and all went ashore for lunch. There was nothing memorable about the lunch in the local cafe.

On returning to the boat, we let go and set off again, heading for Gabo Island and from there to Refuge Cove on Wilsons Promontory. This would be a two day trip, all going well.

We sailed with dolphins for company and rounded the SE corner of Australia, into Victoria in excellent conditions, warm and sunny with gentle breezes. As we neared Lakes Entrance we ran into heavy fog. We were of course under engine in flat seas and no wind. Our only real problem in the fog was that the oil rigs were all around and we only had about 50 metres of visibility. Don't forget there was no working radar on board. We managed not to hit any, although we did take a close look at one of them, deliberately. All are marked on the charts anyway so we knew where they were.

Our plan was to stop at Refuge Cove for a night just to rest but in the end we didn't as the conditions were holding good and I can never refuse good sailing conditions. So in the middle of the night, we rounded the Prom, in between the islands, and out of the shipping track, spending our time peering out looking for the dim navigation lights there. All the time motor-sailing happily towards home and families.

At 1.30 am on the morning of 25 August we set "Otto" to steer directly to Port Phillip Heads, having cleared all the islands safely. The conditions were still flat and peaceful with a starry night and dolphins around. These continued all day, but we were finding it cold! Progress, as always on the final part, seemed slow but we made it to the Heads. We almost hit a small fishing boat on the way, a combination of swell and a setting sun meant that we did not see him, fortunately he saw us coming for him and moved. He was not a happy camper!

At a quarter past six that evening we were secured alongside at Queenscliff Cruising Yacht Club (QCYC) for the night, having negotiated the Heads with the GPS showing about 15 knots over the ground at one stage. There were several ships waiting to enter as we went through. We turned into the cut leading to QCYC after having waited for the ferry to depart. The yacht club is a small yacht club at the southern end of Port Phillip. It was a welcome refuge from the cold with good company, a good fire and with a stationary cooking and eating area.

26 August saw us away from QCYC and having a great sail home to Sandringham Yacht Club and the end of the journey. We tied up at 3.00 pm and, having drunk a few welcome drinks with friends at the dock, adjourned to the bar.

Chapter 13 - Glossary and Addendum

The Yacht BlueFlyer

- A Jeanneau Sun Odyssey 49, built in 2005 in France.
- She has a 3 cabin layout, 2 doubles at the stern and 1 double forward, that is the owners cabin with an en suite shower and toilet, and a second toilet and shower aft.
- Forward of the aft cabin on the starboard side is the chart table with an unusual seating arrangement.
- Port side forward of the shower is the galley area with freezer, fridge, cooker and sinks.
- The boat is 14.76m in length, 4.56m in beam and 2.1m draft with an encapsulated iron keel, and she is a single masted sloop rig with a removable inner forestay for the storm jib.
- Overall fully laden weight is approximately 16 tonnes, light weight approximately 14 tonnes.

Basic Equipment

- VHF (Very High Frequency). This is a short range, line of sight, radio. We had one fixed one with 2 stations on board, and a hand held one that I left on Palmerston.
- HF SSB, (High Frequency, Single Side Band). This is a long range radio, around the world in good conditions. We had 1 on board. Very similar to amateur radio.
- AIS (Automatic Identification System). There are 2 types:

Receive only, and Send and Receive. All commercial vessels over 300 tonnes are supposed to have the second type smaller vessels, including yachts, are also encouraged to have the second type; which we had. The transmitters show up on electronic chart plotters that most people now have. All military vessels are exempt from having to use this equipment.

- Desalinator or Water Maker. This is a high pressure system for extracting almost everything except water from sea water including salt. This leaves a very bland but quite drinkable water supply.
- Generator. This was a 2 cylinder diesel powered unit on board. Made in Italy it was very quiet and produced 5.5 KVA with a remote control panel.
- Engine. The trusty Yanmar was a Japanese engine, built in Holland. Rated output of 100 cv max, driving a 3 blade folding Flex o Fold propeller.
- Sails. We carried a total of 5 on board. The Mainsail, the 130% genoa, a high foot Yankee jib, the storm sail and the gennaker. The sails in use were on 'furlers' for ease of handling, except the gennaker and the orange-coloured storm one which uses the demountable inner forestay. We have never had to use this one!
- Cooker. This was a bottled gas fed unit with 4 burners, an oven and a grill. It was mounted on gimbals so as to take some of the boat motion out when cooking. There are 2 gas bottles in the port quarter locker.
- Chart Plotter. We have the main one at the chart table below deck, and a repeater in the cockpit. These electronic machines use GPS to show the boats position, speed etc on a screen. It also has charts showing land, water depths, hazards, etc as the boat moves. The radar can be superimposed on the chart.
- Autopilot. This amazing crew member, named "Otto", would steer whatever course, or route, set by the crew. He could be overwhelmed by weather conditions and would then switch off. He can also tack the boat and sail to the wind.
- Bow Thruster. This is a small electric, 12 volt motor, with a double propeller fitted in the bow. It's function is to help move the bow sideways. It is not very strong, especially when missing a propeller.

- Fridge. This was installed by the builders in France prior to collection. An air cooled unit, it never gave trouble.
- Freezer. I had this fitted in the Canary Islands. It was originally a cool box next to the fridge. It worked, but not always well. Another air-cooled unit.
- Air Conditioner. This was also fitted by the builders and was also a heater. It ran from either shore power or the generator. It uses sea water and it's filter needed regular cleaning.
- Dive Compressor. I had one fitted before leaving to refill the Scuba diving tanks. It was virtually never used.
- Fuel tanks. We had one main engine only tank of 240 litres. Good for approximately 500 miles under engine, more if the sails were helping. There was also a secondary tank up forward to supply the generator. This held about 90 litres.
- We also carried 12 x 20 litre jerrycans in the stern lockers.
- Life raft. This was a 4 person ocean rated emergency unit. Never used!
- Water. There were 3 plastic tanks on board, 2 under the forward berths and 1 aft. All were 240 litre capacity with a manifold system and usage gauge. We also carried a lot of bottled water for drinking.
- Anchor. A 'Rocna' 33kg unit on 85 metres of 10 mm chain. This was the best anchor I've ever had. We also had on board a plough anchor for the stern and another emergency plough, never used.
- Dinghy. This was an Austral aluminium hulled inflatable. Very tough and never needed pumping. 2.5 metre long, 4 people absolute maximum.
- Outboard. A Mercury 3.5 cv 4 stroke unit. Good and worked well. However both it and the dinghy were too small.
- EPIRB (Emergency Position Indicator Radio Beacon). This is a small radio unit that gives out its geographical position when activated.
- PLB (Personal Locator Beacon). We had 4 of these on board. They slip into a pocket or can be clipped onto a belt.

- Australia
- Indonesia, Lombok Island
- Australia, Christmas Island
- Australia, Cocos (Keeling) Islands
- Mauritius
- France, La Reunion
- South Africa
- Britain, St Helena
- Brazil
- Grenada
- St Lucia
- France, Martinique
- Dominica
- Antigua
- Holland, Sant Maarten
- Tortola/Tortuga
- Dominican Republic
- Anagua
- Cuba
- Jamaica
- Panama
- Colombia, Las Perlas Islands
- Ecuador, Galápagos Islands
- France, Rangiroa
- France, Tahiti
- France, Moorea
- France, Huahine
- France, Raietea
- France, Bora Bora
- Rarotonga
- Palmerston Island
- Tonga, Vava'u
- Fiji, Viti Levu
- France, New Caledonia

Approximate number of sea miles covered was 30,000 over about 2½ years, at a cost never to be worked out!

1. Eric, Sharyn and Meg.
2. Peter, Cheryl, and Bernie.
3. Peter, Cheryl and Shinichi.
4. Peter and Cheryl.
5. Garry and Dawn.
6. Michael M., Jamie, Michael B.
7. Michael, Jamie and John.
8. Michael, Jamie and Judith.
9. Michael and Jamie.
10. Chris, Gabrielle and Graham.
11. Garry, Dawn and Meg.
12. Eric and Amo.

My heartfelt thanks go to them all as this voyage would not have been possible without their help and good humour at all times.

As to the future, who knows, I certainly don't.

Hugh Pilsworth.
(Awaiting boat)

www.ingramcontent.com/pod-product-compliance
Ingram Content Group UK Ltd.
Pitfield, Milton Keynes, MK11 3LW, UK
UKHW062302290726
14090UKWH00017B/835

9 780646 842424